PERFECT IN THEIR ART

POEMS ON BOXING
FROM HOMER TO ALI

Edited by

Robert Hedin and Michael Waters

Foreword by

Budd Schulberg

SOUTHERN ILLINOIS UNIVERSITY PRESS

Carbondale

06 05 04 03   4 3 2 1

Library of Congress Cataloging-in-Publication Data

Perfect in their art : poems on boxing from Homer to Ali / edited by Robert Hedin
and Michael Waters ; foreword by Budd Schulberg.
p. cm.
1. Boxing—Poetry. I. Hedin, Robert, 1949– II. Waters, Michael, 1949–
PN6110.B77P47 2003
808.81′9355—dc21
ISBN 0-8093-2530-6 (alk. paper)
ISBN 0-8093-2531-4 (pbk. : alk. paper)   2003004558

Socrates: And do you suppose, Adeimantus, that a single boxer who was perfect in his art would easily be a match for two stout and well-to-do gentlemen who were not boxers?

—Plato, *The Republic*

. . . he knew, with terrible lucidity, that the sport was for madmen.

—Leonard Gardner, *Fat City*

CONTENTS

FOREWORD

Y OU WOULD have to look long and hard to find any poetry dedicated to football, basketball, track meets, hockey, or polo. Except perhaps for baseball, no sport has inspired such a quantity and quality of poetry as boxing. What a paradox that the most brutal of sports is also one of the most sensitive and the most creative. Small wonder that the poetry in motion of a Willie Pep, a Ray Robinson, an Ali is matched by the written poetry of Maya Angelou and Horace Gregory, of Langston Hughes, Wole Soyinka and Philip Levine. . . . Not to mention Pindar and Virgil, Homer and Plato.

While some may maintain that boxing is not a metaphor for life, the range of the poetry selected in this provocative and entertaining anthology seems to offer a rather eloquent rebuttal. One poet watching the desperate action in the ring sees the desperate battle with his overmatched wife in the grimy ring of their marriage. Another sees an old black fighter as doing battle for his race against centuries of oppression. A third sees boxing as the ultimate test of pride and character and human dignity. Poetry breathes metaphors as lungs do air. These are poems we want to go back and reread because the more they tell us about boxing, the more they tell us about the human condition. I remember listening to that dedicated monk of boxing, the trainer/manager Cus D'Amato, who taught both his champions and young hopefuls that far more important than the physical conflict was the power of the mind. "It's fistic character that wins fights," he insisted, and I always felt he inspired his boys to go beyond Stallone's "eye of the tiger" to the eye of the poet.

After getting knocked out in the ring, the battered poet Charley Bukowski wrote:

> . . . I got up and dressed,
> the tape still on my hands, and when I got home
> I tore the tape off my hands and

wrote my first poem,
and I've been fighting
ever since.

That identification of one discipline with another is a telling sum-up of the attraction so many good writers have felt toward fighters. Not so surprisingly, they become interchangeable. Ali recites his saucy dog-gerel and Hemingway misses with a roundhouse punch and dreams of being heavyweight champion of the world. It is both to our glory and self-doubt that we see ourselves eternally vulnerable and challenged in life's ring, and sigh a "me-too" to the distinguished poet James Merrill's "The Seventh Round":

> *Give it to him!*
> To you, you mean.
> As always (mezzanine
> Gone dazzling dim,
>
> A crown at stake)
> Before you stands
> The giver with clenched hands.
> Drop your own. Take.

But there are upbeat ballads singing the praises of our heroes, the Black and White Jacks, Johnson and Dempsey, Louis and Ali; the folk singers Leadbelly, Bob Dylan, and Paul Simon weigh in too, while Langston Hughes and Richard Wright lead the cheers for the Brown Bomber, our twentieth century John Henry, who "knocked out Hitler" when he whupped Max Schmeling. Now don't tell me that was no metaphor. Our Joe sends their Max to the hospital in round one. A two-minute epic. And we win World War II. Just like that. With gifted poets to sing it down the years.

There are blues here for the game dead Benny Paret. There are more losers than winners. Life is a very tough ring. There are the leaden eyes of our "baddest nigger" Sonny Liston who, in the poetic words of his press agent, "died the day he was born." There is the rhymed re-quiem for the protagonist of Joseph Moncure March's memorable book-length poem, *The Setup*, effectively excerpted here. The poets don't devote immortal lines to polo or ping pong. They reserve their art for the life-and-death experiences of pugilistica. The poets are fighters. And the fighters are poets.

Box on. Read on . . .

BUDD SCHULBERG
Brookside
Quiogue, New York

INTRODUCTION

BOXING IS one of the oldest forms of human competition. Dating back four thousand years, the sport has been memorialized on the walls of tombs at Beni Hasan in Egypt and in the decorative frescoes excavated on Akrotiri (now Santorini, thought by some to be the site of legendary Atlantis). Boxing has been celebrated in epinician odes and epic poems of classical Greece and Rome, and even makes a brief but spirited appearance in Plato's dialogue, *The Republic*.

Perfect in Their Art presents poems written about the sport of boxing from ancient to modern times. Comprised of more than one hundred of the finest poems from both oral and written traditions, the volume celebrates the literary, historical, and cultural significance of what many sport historians consider the purest, most elemental form of athleticism. Gathered are poems by such classical poets as Homer, Virgil, and Pindar, as well as selections by nineteenth- and twentieth-century poets—some of whom fought in the ring—from England, Ireland, and the United States, among other nations. The volume also includes poems by prizefighters, trainers, referees, and sportswriters and a rich sampling of unique musical lyrics and scores. Displaying a wide range of themes, attitudes, and perspectives, *Perfect in Their Art* offers glimpses into boxing's storied history, its facts and fables, its social and cultural impact (the first sport to be filmed was boxing, in 1894), as well as insights into the many gifted individuals whose virtuosity in the ring (and sometimes on the page) has helped make the sport memorable for countless generations of fight fans.

For many of the poets in this volume, boxing is far more than a simple, elemental sport. For some, such as Horace Gregory, David Ignatow, and John Skoyles, it remains the great social equalizer, the ring acting as a place where such traits as character and endurance often overcome wealth and social status. For other poets, it evokes the struggle for racial equality. In poems such as "Joe Louis" by Langston Hughes, "Baby Villon" by Philip Levine, and "A Dream of the Ring:

The Great Jack Johnson" by George Barlow, the boxing ring becomes a symbolic stage where America's ongoing racial struggles are played out on an allegorical level. Still other poets in the volume view boxing as a means to bolster a nation's self-image. Both "Champ Joe Louis" by "Little Bill" Gaither and "A Ballad of the Life and Times of Joe Louis" by Calvin Hernton, for example, deal with the famous 1937 battle between Louis and German heavyweight Max Schmeling, a fight that Louis won in two minutes and four seconds of the first round and one that was quickly seized upon by the public as a supreme vindication of America's democratic ideals at a time when European fascism was on the rise.

A great many of the poems in *Perfect in Their Art* devote themselves to the sport's more memorable battles. Homer, in an excerpt from the *Iliad* included here, describes in rich detail the fight between Epeious and Euralos, while the challenge of Dares is graphically depicted by Virgil in a section of the *Aeneid* also included. The volume also presents two of Pindar's odes, both written for the early Olympic games some twenty-five hundred years ago. Of considerable literary and historical importance, these are some of the only surviving poems from the classical world that provide not only a glimpse of boxing's early bouts but also a sense of the nearly mythical status afforded boxers during that period. In addition, other poets—William Makepeace Thackeray, John Masefield, Elizabeth Alexander, and Yusef Komunyakaa—depict the monumental battles between such fighters as Sayer and Heenan, Johnson and Burns, and Dempsey and Firpo. All attempt, through their own art, to reanimate the sport's most defining moments, to remind us again how truly exhilarating such moments can be.

Perfect in Their Art also includes poems dealing with some of the game's greatest heroes, fighters who earned their place in the sport's pantheon, who seemed to transcend, through skill and character, grace and virtuosity, through sheer moxie, the limitations of the flesh, if only for a few moments. Jack Johnson, Jack Dempsey, Joe Louis, and Muhammad Ali are a few of the boxers celebrated in this volume, all champions who symbolized their respective eras and who were embraced by a public wanting some share in their triumphs. Of the great eighteenth- and nineteenth-century fighters, James Figg, Jack Randall, and John L. Sullivan, among others, are honored for their exploits. Of special note is "British Lads and Black Millers" by prizefighter Bob Gregson, a poem about Tom Molineaux, an ex-slave from Virginia who gained wide renown in England in the nineteenth century. It is perhaps the first poem ever written in which a boxer of African American heritage is mentioned.

Without doubt, some of the most poignant pieces in *Perfect in Their Art* deal with fighters who have been forced by age or injury into retirement. There is the aging John L. Sullivan in John Hildebidle's "Relics," for example, who spends his last days pruning his arbor trees, a "ham-fisted, barrelbellied monument" to his former self. Or Joe Louis in David Spicer's eponymous poem who has lost his legendary "steam-hammer punch" and whom Spicer depicts as an "old man / boxed in by loneliness." Or the retired fighter in Jeffrey Skinner's "Closed-Head Wounds" who still jogs every morning, "though not so early / as before, not so fast." Indeed, such poems remind us that however brutal boxing may be, life outside the ring, for these fighters, seems empty, lacking purpose. Still other poems—"To a Fighter Killed in the Ring" by Lou Lipsitz and "Blues for Benny 'Kid' Paret" by Dave Smith—recall the specter of death that looms over every match. In addition, the volume includes several moving epitaphs to Daniel Donnelly, Jack Randall, and other early heroes of the ring in England and Ireland.

A number of poets in *Perfect in Their Art*—Jack Driscoll, Page Dougherty, Richard Foerster, Natasha Trethewey, among others—offer personal and intimate testimonies to boxing's hold on their lives. Filled with memorable details, their poems tell of learning to box, of watching the Friday Night Fights in the early days of the television age, or of growing up in an era when boxing, despite its seamy underside, was considered an honorable sport, what the *New Yorker* staff reporter A. J. Liebling termed "the Sweet Science," one filled with discipline and moral fortitude and artful enough to be passed down from parents to children, one generation to another.

Also included in the volume is a rich sampling of boxing music—early milling songs, ballads, blues, marches, waltzes, and contemporary pop lyrics. Some, such as "You Valiant Sons of Erin's Isle" by an anonymous writer and "The Feats of Prime Jack Randall, O!" by Pierce Egan, are good examples of nineteenth-century Irish and British milling songs. Rising out of boxing clubs, pubs, and early working class tabloids, they are typically adulatory in tone and tend to portray their subjects as part of a long legacy of heroic figures, praised for their strength and skill, as well as for their ability to uphold moral virtue and national pride. Others, such as "Champ Joe Louis" by "Little Bill" Gaither, "Winner Joe (The Knock-Out King)" by Lil Johnson, and "He's in the Ring" by Memphis Minnie, all popular blues songs of the 1930s and 1940s, extol similar qualities and suggest how champions like Louis were able to achieve iconic status in the United States. In addition, *Perfect in Their Art* includes a rare reproduction of the music and lyrics for a popular song from the 1920s—"'Angel Firpo' Waltz" by Salomon Pacorah—as well as lyrics by contemporary songwriters such as Bob Dylan, Paul Simon, and Warren Zevon, lyrics that extend the tradition of boxing music to the present.

The poems in *Perfect in Their Art* have been placed in alphabetical order, and no attempt has been made to create any artificial divisions between oral and written poetries. This has been done in hopes that poems from different eras, cultural milieux, and literary traditions will overlap in theme and sensibility, one shedding light upon the other, lending all a fuller meaning. Together, the selections evoke the unique history and spirit of boxing and, in the process, allow many of its greatest heroes, those who elevated the sport to a level of grace and beauty, to step once more into the ring, lean and hungry and back in their prime, their spotlighted robes flaring again in the air.

ROBERT HEDIN
Red Wing, Minnesota

MICHAEL WATERS
Salisbury, Maryland

Perfect in Their Art

Late Round

KIM ADDONIZIO

When the fighters slow down, moving towards each other
as though underwater, gloves laboring to rise
before their faces, each punch followed by a clutch
when they hold on like exhausted lovers,
I think of us in the last months, and of the night
you stood in my kitchen, drunk, throwing wild combinations
at the air, at something between us that would not
go down. I watch the two of them
planted in that ring, unable to trust their legs,
the bell's reprieve suspended in some impossible distance,
and I remember my voice, cursing our life together
until there was nothing either one of us would fight for.
These men, you'd say, have heart—they keep on,
though neither remembers his strategy
or hears the shouts from his corner. And it's true
you had more heart than I did, until that night
you gave us up, finally, and dropped crying to your knees
on my kitchen floor. The fighters stagger and fall together,
flailing against the ropes. They embrace
and are separated, but they don't let go.

The Shadowboxer

Ai

You know what hunger is, Father,
it's the soothing half-dark
of the library men's room
and the reference librarian,
his head pressed against my thigh
as tears run down his pudgy face.
Sometimes I unzip for him
and let him look,
but never touch, never taste.
After all, I'm here to try to reconcile
the classics
with the Batman-comics philosophy of life,
and this pathetic masquerade,
this can't be life in caps or even lower case.
This is 1955, and all I know is boredom and desire,
so when I leave, I cruise down Main Street
for girls and a quick feel.
They call it the ugliest street in America,
but I don't know yet
that it's just another in a lifetime of streets
that end kissing somebody's feet or ass.
I just tell myself to drive and keep on driving,
but like always, I swerve into our yard.
You're still at Henrahan's,
drunk and daring anyone to hit you,
because you're a man goddamnit.
I climb the stairs to my room
and lie down under your boxing gloves,
hung above my bed
since your last fight in Havana.
When I can't sleep,
I take them down, put them on,
and shadowbox, until I swing,

lose my balance, and fall,
and on the count of six
you rise off the canvas,
only to be knocked backward into the ropes,
sure that half your face
flew out of the ring,
but it was only blood flung
like so much rum from a glass
into all the screaming faces,
into one woman's face
as she stands
and leans into the next spray of blood.
Do it, she cries
as she raises her fists, *do it.*
Bathed, stitched, and taped together,
you manage to dress
and get halfway to the street door
before you feel her
behind you in the darkness primeval,
but when you call, nobody answers
and you're twelfth floor up
Hotel Delirious
with Billie Holiday on the hi-fi.
Don't explain, she sings,
and the rum on the night table,
for the sweet dreams
it never really does bring, sings back, *Do,*
as you perform your latest attempt
to escape you, Father,
and what happened one night
when I stopped believing
even in the power of money to absolve.
Remember?
The first time I had a woman,
I even called your name. You didn't answer,
but you do answer the three short knocks,
and my mother, Rose,
still wearing her blood-spattered clothes,

crosses the threshold.
Turn back before it's too late, I tell her,
as she peels the tape off your face,
licks and kisses your wounds,
then mounts you
and plunges you deeper each time,
crying, *Show me what a good man can do,*
and you, Father, you,
rocking with her
until you must slow her, must ease her off
and stanch the blood above your eye.
Can you feel me, Father, breaking into a run
down conception road,
nothing but nasty business on my mind,
just two steps ahead
of all the bloody noses,
the broken bones
and blackened eyes you'll give me?
Nobody believes the lies you tell,
but they want to
and that's enough.
It's tough without a mother,
but fatherless is tougher on a boy, they say.
Nobody sees how twisted up I am
or how squeezed dry of anything resembling love.
I loved my mother,
but she left us to our few feet of deep space
for the hard chest and thighs of a comer,
the postcards she sent now and then from Venezuela,
Australia, even Paris,
reminding you of what you want to forget,
and when your good eye lingers on your son,
all you see is one more reason to hit him.

Then one night, you stagger to my room.
I don't resist when you slap and kick me.
Faggot, you scream

as you tear my T-shirt and shorts off me,
I heard about the library.
Then, then, you rape me.
You're snoring when I pack my gym bag
and take the boxing gloves
and stuff them in with my underwear
and Old Spice soap-on-a-rope.
I don't know where I'm going,
I just go as far as I can,
which in the end is Bellevue Detox,
is suddenly the smell of Gleason's gym—
men's sweat,
men's armpits, crotches,
men's wins and losses,
all that's left of Rosy Jack, Jack Rose,
middleweight loser
and sometime trainer of other losers mostly
or movie stars
and novelists who think the fights are glamorous,
who want to get in touch with themselves
by hitting someone else,
or for a "serious" role,
but I tell them
it's really all about a boy
finally beaten to submission.
Although he's crying *More,*
because he's been taught to think
he deserves to be punished,
he doesn't hear himself
as he locks the door
to keep his father in the wretched past
where he belongs,
but the past is now,
is you, Father, in this corner
and me in mine, stripped
to your level at last,
as the bell sounds

and the crowd bites down
on its collective tongue,
when the first punch stuns me
and the second knocks me all the way
to kingdom come and gone.

Narrative: Ali

ELIZABETH ALEXANDER

a poem in twelve rounds

1.

My head so big
they had to pry
me out. I'm sorry
Bird (is what I call
my mother). Cassius
Marcellus Clay,
Muhammad Ali;
you can say
my name in any
language, any
continent: Ali.

2.

Two photographs
of Emmett Till,
born my year,
on my birthday.
One, he's smiling,
happy, and the other one
is after. His mother
did the bold thing,
kept the casket open
made the thousands look upon
his bulging eyes,
his twisted neck,
her lynched black boy.
I couldn't sleep
for thinking,
Emmett Till.

One day I went
down to the train tracks,
found some iron
shoe-shine rests
and planted them
between the ties
and waited
for a train to come,
and watched the train
derail, and ran,
and after that
I slept at night.

3.
I need to train
around people,
hear them talk,
talk back. I need
to hear the traffic,
see people in
the barbershop,
people getting
shoe shines, talking,
hear them talk,
talk back.

4.
Bottom line: Olympic gold
can't buy a black man
a Louisville hamburger
in nineteen-sixty.

Wasn't even real gold.
I watched the river
drag the ribbon down,
red, white, and blue.

5.
Laying on the bed,
praying for a wife,
in walk Sonji Roi.

Pretty little shape.
Do you like
chop suey?

Can I wash your hair
underneath
that wig?

Lay on the bed,
Girl. Lie
with me.

Shake to the east,
to the north,
south, west—

but remember,
remember, I need
a Muslim wife. So

Quit using lipstick.
Quit your boogaloo.
Cover up your knees

like a Muslim
wife, religion,
religion, a Muslim

wife. Eleven
months with Sonji,
first woman I loved.

6.
There's not
too many days
that pass that I
don't think
of how it started,
but I know
no Great White Hope
can beat
a true black champ.
Jerry Quarry
could have been
a movie star,
a millionaire,
a senator,
a president—
he only had
to do one thing,
is whip me,
but he can't.

7. *Dressing-Room Visitor*
He opened
up his shirt:
"KKK" cut
in his chest.
He dropped
his trousers:
latticed scars
where testicles
should be. His face
bewildered, frozen,
in the Alabama woods
that night in 1966
when they left him
for dead, his testicles
in a Dixie cup.
You a warning,

they told him,
to smart-mouth,
sassy-acting niggers,
meaning niggers
still alive,
meaning any nigger,
meaning niggers
like me.

8. *TRAINING*
Unsweetened grapefruit juice
will melt my stomach down.
Don't drive if you can walk,
don't walk if you can run.
I add a mile each day
and run in eight-pound boots.

My knuckles sometimes burst
the glove. I let dead skin
build up, and then I peel it,
let it scar, so I don't bleed
as much. My bones
absorb the shock.

I train in three-minute
spurts, like rounds: three
rounds big bag, three speed
bag, three jump rope, one-
minute breaks,
no more, no less.

Am I too old? Eat only
kosher meat. Eat cabbage,
carrots, beets, and watch
the weight come down:
two-thirty, two-twenty,
two-ten, two-oh-nine.

9.
Will I go
like Kid Paret,
a fractured
skull, a ten-day
sleep, dreaming
alligators, pork
chops, saxophones,
slow grinds, funk,
fishbowls, lightbulbs,
bats, typewriters,
tuning forks, funk,
clocks, red rubber
ball, what you see
in that lifetime
knockout minute
on the cusp?
You could be
let go,
you could be
snatched back.

10. *RUMBLE IN THE JUNGLE*
Ali boma ye,
Ali boma, ye,
means kill him, Ali,
which is different
from a whupping
which is what I give,
but I lead them chanting
anyway, *Ali*
boma ye, because
here in Africa
black people fly
planes and run countries.

I'm still making up
for the foolishness

I said when I was
Clay from Louisville,
where I learned Africans
lived naked in straw
huts eating tiger meat,
grunting and grinning,
swinging from vines,
pounding their chests—

I pound my chest but of my own accord.

    II.

I said to Joe Frazier,
first thing, get a good house
in case you get crippled
so you and your family
can sleep somewhere. Always
keep one good Cadillac.
And watch how you dress
with that cowboy hat,
pink suits, white shoes—
that's how pimps dress,
or kids, and you a champ,
or wish you were, 'cause
I can whip you in the ring
or whip you in the street.
Now back to clothes,
wear dark clothes, suits,
black suits, like you the best
at what you do, like you
President of the World.
Dress like that.
Put them yellow pants away.
We dinosaurs gotta
look good, gotta sound
good, gotta be good,
the greatest, that's what
I told Joe Frazier,

and he said to me,
we both bad niggers.
We don't do no crawlin'.

12.
They called me "the fistic pariah."

They said I didn't love my country,
called me a race-hater, called me out
of my name, waited for me
to come out on a stretcher, shot at me,
hexed me, cursed me, wished me
all manner of ill will,
told me I was finished.

Here I am,
like the song says,
come and take me,

"The People's Champ,"

myself,
Muhammad.

Today's News

ELIZABETH ALEXANDER

Heavyweight champion of the world Mike Tyson
broke his fist in a street brawl in Harlem
at three A.M. outside an all-night clothing store
where he was buying an 800-dollar, white
leather coat. The other dude, on TV, said,
"It was a sucker punch." Muhammad Ali said
Tyson ain't pretty enough to be heavyweight
champion of the world. Years ago a new Ali
threw his Olympic gold into the Ohio
River, said he'd get it when black people were truly
free in this country. In South Africa there is a dance
that says we are fed up we have no work you have
struck a rock. I saw it on today's news.

I didn't want to write a poem that said "blackness
is," because we know better than anyone
that we are not one or ten or ten thousand things
Not one poem We could count ourselves forever
and never agree on the number. When the first
black Olympic gymnast was black and on TV I called
home to say it was colored on channel three
in nineteen eighty-eight. Most mornings these days
Ralph Edwards comes into the bedroom and says, "Elizabeth,
this is your life. Get up and look for color,
look for color everywhere."

Clay Comes Out to Meet Liston

MUHAMMAD ALI

Recited by Cassius Clay
Written by Gary Belkin

Clay comes out to meet Liston
And Liston starts to retreat
If Liston goes back any further
He'll end up in a ringside seat
Clay swings with a left
Clay swings with a right
Look at young Cassius
Carry the fight.
Liston keeps backing
But there's not enough room
It's a matter of time
Ere Clay lowers the boom.
Now Clay swings with a right
What a beautiful swing
And the punch raises the bear
Clear out of the ring.
Liston is still rising
And the ref wears a frown
For he can't start counting
Till Sonny comes down.
Now Liston disappears from view
The crowd is getting frantic
But our radar stations have picked him up
He's somewhere over the Atlantic.
Who would have thought
When they came to the fight
That they'd witness the launching
Of a human satellite.
Yes, the crowd did not dream

When they lay down their money
That they would see
A total eclipse of the Sonny.
I am the greatest!

Fightin' Was Natural

MAYA ANGELOU

Fightin' was natural,
hurtin' was real,
and the leather like lead
on the end of my arm
was a ticket to ride
to the top of the hill.
   Fightin' was real.

The sting of the ointment
and scream of the crowd
for blood in the ring,
and the clangin' bell cuttin'
clean through the
cloud in my ears.
   Boxin' was real.

The rope at my back
and the pad on the floor,
the smack of four hammers
new bones in my jaw,
the guard in my mouth,
my tongue startin' to swell.
Fightin' was livin'.
Boxin' was real.
Fightin' was real.
   Livin' was . . . hell.

Epitaph

ANONYMOUS

Underneath this pillar high
Lies Sir Daniel Donnelly,
He was a stout and handy man
And people called him 'Buffing Dan',
Knighthood he took from George's sword
And well he wore it, by my word!
He died at last, from forty-seven
Tumblers of punch he drank one even;

Overthrown by punch, unharmed by fist,
He dies, unbeaten pugilist!
Such a buffer as Donnelly
Ireland never again will see.

Hallowed Ground

ANONYMOUS

A crowd stood near this copse
   A hundred years ago.
On springy turf a roped-of square
Was waiting for a fight most fair,
And Squires with their whips were there
   To cheer 'bold Bendigo'.

'Nottingham Lambs' with sticks and clubs
   Watch while their champion strips,
Appraising as the noises halt
Ribs muscled firm without a fault,
Fists steeled by vinegar and salt—
   A greyhound in the slips.

Alone the birds the silence break,
   A boxer toes the mark.
Eleven stone six of sinewed might
Has trained by day and dreamed by night
Of Ecstasy, the perfect fight,
   Life's triumph, Beauty stark.

To-day Spring tints the little copse
   Unearthly shades of green.
The turf treads firm beneath the feet;
The pulse throbs with a quicker beat;
For on this hallowed ground and sweet
   A perfect fight has been.

I Went Down Last Tuesday Night

ANONYMOUS

I went down last Tuesday night
To see Joe Louis and Max Baer fight
When Joe Louis socked, Max Baer rocked
Dream of a viper
Yeah man, Tee man
Dream of a viper

The Kid's Last Fight

ANONYMOUS

The roaring crowds at the ringside always know that every fight might be a kid's last. Death or glory, or a career cutting out paper dolls, awaits them all.

Us two was pals, the Kid and me;
'Twould cut no ice if some gayzee,
As tough as hell, jumped either one,
We'd both light in and hand him some.

Both of a size, the Kid and me,
We tipped the scales at thirty-three;
And when we'd spar 'twas give and take,
I wouldn't slug for any stake.

One day we worked out at the gym,
Some swell guy hangin' round called "Slim"
Watched us and got stuck on the Kid,
Then signed him up, that's what he did.

This guy called "Slim" he owned a string
Of lightweights, welters, everything;
He took the Kid out on the road,
And where they went none of us knowed.

I guessed the Kid had changed his name,
And fightin' the best ones in the game.
I used to dream of him at night,
No letters came—he couldn't write.

In just about two months or three
I signed up with Bucktooth McGee.
He got me matched with Denver Brown,
I finished him in half a round.

Next month I fought with Brooklyn Mike,
As tough a boy who hit the pike,

Then Frisco Jim and Battlin' Ben,
And knocked them all inside of ten.

I took 'em all and won each bout,
None of them birds could put me out;
The sportin' writers watched me slug,
Then all the papers run my mug.

"He'd rather fight than eat," they said,
"He's got the punch, he'll knock 'em dead."
There's only one I hadn't met,
That guy they called "The Yorkshire Pet."

He'd cleaned 'em all around in France,
No one in England stood a chance;
And I was champ in U.S.A.,
And knocked 'em cuckoo every day.

Now all McGee and me could think
Was how we'd like to cross the drink,
And knock this bucko for a row,
And grab a wagon load of dough.

At last Mac got me matched all right,
Five thousand smackers for the fight;
Then me and him packed up our grip,
And went to grab that championship.

I done some trainin' and the night
Set for the battle sure was right;
The crowd was wild, for this here bout
Was set to last till one was out.

The mob went crazy when the Pet
Came in, I'd never seen him yet;
And then I climbed up through the ropes,
All full of fight and full of hopes.

The crowd gave me an awful yell,
('Twas even money at the bell)
They stamped their feet and shook the place;
The Pet turned 'round, I saw his face!

My guts went sick, that's what they did,
For Holy Gee, it was the Kid!
We just had time for one good shake,
We meant it, too, it wasn't fake.

Whang? went the bell, the fight was on,
I clinched until the round was gone,
A-beggin', that he'd let me take
The fall for him—he wouldn't fake.

Hell, no, the Kid was on the square,
And said we had to fight it fair,
The crowd had bet their dough on us—
We had to fight (the honest cuss).

The referee was yellin', "Break,"
The crowd was sore and howlin', "Fake."
They'd paid their dough to see a scrap,
And so far we'd not hit a tap.

The second round we both begin.
I caught a fast one on my chin;
And stood like I was in a doze,
Until I got one on the nose.

I started landin' body blows,
He hooked another on my nose,
That riled my fightin' blood like hell,
And we was sluggin' at the bell.

The next round started, from the go
The millin' we did wasn't slow,

I landed hard on him, and then,
He took the count right up to ten.

He took the limit on one knee,
A chance to get his wind and see;
At ten he jumped up like a flash
And on my jaw he hung a smash.

I'm fightin', too, there, toe to toe,
And hittin' harder, blow for blow,
I damn soon knowed he couldn't stay,
He rolled his eyes—you know the way.

The way he staggered made me sick,
I stalled, McGee yelled, "Cop him quick."
The crowd was wise and yellin', "Fake,"
They'd seen the chance I wouldn't take.

The mob kept tellin' me to land,
And callin' things I couldn't stand;
I stepped in close and smashed his chin,
The kid fell hard; he was all in.

I carried him into his chair,
And tried to bring him to for fair,
I rubbed his wrists, done everything,
A doctor climbed into the ring.

And I was scared as I could be,
The Kid was starin' and couldn't see;
The doctor turned and shook his head;
I looked again—the Kid was dead!

Parody on Part of Gray's "Elegy in a Churchyard"

ANONYMOUS

Perhaps in this sequester'd spot may dwell
   Some unknown Champion, of true game and breed,
Well skill'd in hitting right and left to tell,
   And parrying desp'rate blows with caution'd heed;

Some village Randall, that, with dauntless breast,
   The light-weight millers of his fields subdued;
Some Martin, yet by Turner uncaress'd;
   Some Cribb, that never tapp'd a Snow-ball's blood.

But knowledge to their eyes his muffled tools,
   Rich with the claret's tinge, did ne'er unfold:
Poor Johnny Raws! nor Belcher's scienced rules,
   Nor Eales' gay set-to, to them were told.

The applause of gay Corinthians to command,
   The chancery suit and fibbing to despise,
At the Fives' Court in proud array to stand,
   The mark for kids' and swells' attentive eyes.

Their lot forbade; nor circumscribed alone
   Their powers of milling—but their cash confined;
Forbade to make the rich prize-purse their own,
   Or hedge the dubious bet with skill refined.

Far from the London Ring's exalted strife,
   In casual loose turns-up they pass'd the day;
Nor Egan's sporting page records their life,
   Nor Gregson chaunts for them his laureate lay.

Yet these green-horns, from insult to protect,
   Their brawny arms in act of letting fly,

With ruffian ire, by art's nice rules uncheck'd,
    Attract the notice of the passer by.

Their peepers, damaged by the unscienced hand,
    The place of feint and skilful stop supply;
While ranged around them stand the rustic band,
    And, gazing, learn their pluck in turn to try.

For, where's the dunghill cur so void of stuff,
    Who manhood's hardy trial e'er resign'd,
Utter'd with faltering tongue the word—Enough,
    Nor cast one longing, lingering look back?

Still on some fav'rite hit the arm relies,
    Some ruby drops the closing eye requires;
E'en 'mid these shades the champion's spirit flies,
    And rustics glow with pugilistic fires.

You Valiant Sons of Erin's Isle

ANONYMOUS

You valiant Sons of Erin's Isle,
  And sweet Columbia too,
Come, gather 'round, and listen while
  I chant a stave for you.
Oh! Fill your glass up, every man,
  With Irish whiskey, stout;
And drink to John L. Sullivan,
  The famous "Knocker-out."

> *Chorus:*
> Oh! The chorus swell for bold John L.,
> We'll fling it to the breeze,
> Yes, shout it loud, so England's crowd
> Shall hear it o'er the seas;
> The great and small, he's downed them all
> In many a clever bout;
> Hurray for John L. Sullivan,
> The famous "Knocker-out."

They sent men here from England's shore,
  The best they could produce,
The great John L. to try and floor,
  but 'twasn't any use.
Try how they would, they never could
  Give Sullivan the rout,
For like a giant there he stood,
  This famous "Knocker-out. . . . "

A Dream of the Ring: The Great Jack Johnson

GEORGE BARLOW

I'll be the first
to chase the white hope
from coast to coast
corner him at last
& buckle his knees
Rednecks in Reno
will check in their guns
& drop their ducats
to watch the sun gleam
from my teeth my dark muscles
my great bald head
Vamps & debs will blush & giggle
as they watch me train
will prance into paradise with me
carve their lives in my back
fan themselves
knead my heart like dough
Hate will snag me
jail me for crossing state lines
& being a man
I'll fight bulls in Madrid
Griots will feed me to their children
to make them strong
My jabs & hooks
sweat & knockouts
my derbies long cars & gall
will live forever
I'll have one rag of a time
when I become Jack Johnson

That's What the Well-Dressed Man in Harlem Will Wear

IRVING BERLIN

Production Number from *This Is the Army*

There's a change in fashion that shows
In the Lenox Avenue clothes;
Mister Dude has disappeared with his flashy tie;
You'll see in the Harlem *Esquire*
What the well-dressed man will desire
When he's struttin' down the street with his sweetie pie.

Suntan shade of cream
Or an olive drab color scheme—
That's what the well-dressed man in Harlem will wear.
Dressed up in OD's
With a tin hat for overseas—
That's what the well-dressed man in Harlem will wear.
Top hat, white tie and tails no more,
They've been put away till after the war.
If you want to know,
Take a look at Brown Bomber Joe—
That's what the well-dressed man in Harlem will wear.

The Boxing Lesson

RICHARD BRODERICK

"Keep it light, boys. Keep it light,"
my father would shout from the sidelines,
meaning light on our feet, dancing and circling,
never coming in direct at your opponent,
like that time my youngest brother
walked right into my straight-armed left
and knocked himself flat.

It was as if his sons were figures
in a myth whose feet might take root
the instant we stopped moving,
a suit of chainmail bark creeping up
over our thighs and trunks, freezing
us in place so we'd end up reeling
punchdrunk before the fists of any breeze.

If, as he taught us to, I look for movement
out of the corner of my eye
("The punch you don't see coming
is the one you've got to watch for"),
I can glimpse him out there in the blue arena,
dancing and circling, always moving,
as he boxes Death himself,
snapping back the hooded head
with a crisp one-two.

Crispus Attucks McKoy

STERLING A. BROWN

I sing of a hero,
Unsung, unrecorded,
Known by the name
Of Crispus Attucks McKoy,
Born, bred in Boston,
Stepson of Garvey,
Cousin of Trotter,
Godson of Du Bois.

No monastic hairshirt
Stung flesh more bitterly
Than the white coat
In which he was arrayed;
But what was his agony
On entering the drawing-room
To hear a white woman
Say slowly, "One spade."

He threw up his job,
His scorn was sublime,
And he left the bridge party
Simply aghast;
Lo, see him striding
Out of the front door
A free man again
His infamy past.

Down at the Common,
The cradle of freedom,
Another shock nearly
Carried him away
Someone called out "Shine"
And he let loose a blue streak,

And the poor little bootblack
Slunk frightened away.

In a bakery window
He read with a glance
"Brown Betties for sale"
And his molars gnashed;
Up came the kerbstone,
Back went his trusty arm,
Swift was his gesture,
The plate glass was smashed.

On the sub, Crispus
Could have committed murder,
Mayhem and cannibalism,
When he heard a maid
Say to the cherub
Opposite to her,
"Come over here, darling,
Here's a little shade."

But down at the Gardens,
He knew was his refuge,
Recompense for insults,
Solace for grief,
A Negro battler,
Slugging Joe Johnson
Was fighting an Irishman
Battling Dan O'Keefe.

The garden was crammed,
Mickeys, Kikes, Bohunks,
Polacks and Dagoes,
All over the place,
Crispus strode in,
Regally, boldly,
The sole representative
Of his race.

The fight was even,
When Joey hit Dan,
The heart of Crispus
Shone with a steady glow,
When Dan hit Joey,
Crispus groaned "foul,"
"Oh the dirty low-down
So-and-so."

In the tenth round,
Dan got to swinging,
Joey was dazed,
And clinched and held,
When suddenly,
Right behind Crispus,
"Kill the Nigger!"
Somebody yelled.

Crispus got up
In all of his fury;
Lightning bolts zigzagged
Out of his eyes,
With a voice like thunder
He blurted his challenge,
"Will the bastard who said that
Please arise."

Thirty-five thousand
Nordics and Alpines,
Hebrews and Gentiles,
As one man arose,
See how our hero,
Armed with his noble cause,
Armed with righteousness
To battle goes.

They found an ankle in Dedham,
A thighbone in Maldon,

An elbow in Somerville,
Both nostrils in Lynn,
And on Boston Common
Lay one of his eyebrows,
The cap of his knee,
And a piece of his shin.

Peabody Museum
Has one of his eardrums;
His sound heart was found
In Lexington;
But over the reaches
From Cape Cod to Frisco
The soul of our hero
Goes marching on . . .

Strange Legacies

STERLING A. BROWN

One thing you left with us, Jack Johnson.
One thing before they got you.

You used to stand there like a man,
Taking punishment
With a golden, spacious grin;
Confident.
Inviting big Jim Jeffries, who was boring in:
"Heah ah is, big boy; yuh sees whah Ise at.
Come on in . . ."

Thanks, Jack, for that.

John Henry, with your hammer;
John Henry, with your steel driver's pride,
You taught us that a man could go down like a man,
Sticking to your hammer till you died.
Sticking to your hammer till you died.

Brother,
When, beneath the burning sun
The sweat poured down and the breath came thick,
And the loaded hammer swung like a ton
And the heart grew sick;
You had what we need now, John Henry.
Help us get it.

So if we go down
Have to go down
We go like you, brother,
Nachal' men . . .

Old nameless couple in Red River Bottom,
Who have seen floods gutting out your best loam,
And the boll weevil chase you
Out of your hard-earned home,
Have seen the drought parch your green fields,
And the cholera stretch your porkers out dead;
Have seen year after year
The commissary always a little in the lead;
Even you said
That which we need
Now in our time of fear,—
Routed your own deep misery and dread,
Muttering, beneath an unfriendly sky,
"Guess we'll give it one mo' try.
Guess we'll give it one mo' try."

the loser

CHARLES BUKOWSKI

and the next I remembered I'm on a table,
everybody's gone; the head of bravery
under light, scowling, flailing me down . . .
and then some toad stood there, smoking a cigar:
"Kid you're no fighter," he told me,
and I got up and knocked him over a chair;
it was like a scene in a movie, and
he stayed there on his big rump and said
over and over: "Jesus, Jesus, whatsamatta wit
you?" and I got up and dressed,
the tape still on my hands, and when I got home
I tore the tape off my hands and
wrote my first poem,
and I've been fighting
ever since.

From *Letters and Journals*

GEORGE GORDON, LORD BYRON

November 24, 1813—Just returned from dinner with Jackson (the Emperor of Pugilism) and another of the select, at Crib's the champion's. I drank more than I like, and have brought away some three bottles of very fair claret—for I have no headache. We had Tom —— up after dinner; very facetious, though somewhat prolix. He don't like his situation—wants to fight again—pray Pollux (or Castor, if he was the *miller)* he may! Tom has been a sailor—a coal heaver—and some other genteel profession, before he took to the cestus. Tom has been in action at sea, and is now only three-and-thirty. A great man! has a wife and a mistress, and conversations well—bating some sad omissions and misapplications of the aspirate. Tom is an old friend of mine; I have seen some of his best battles in my nonage. He is now a publican, and, I fear, a sinner—for Mrs. —— is on alimony, and ——'s daughter lives with the champion. This —— told me; Tom, having an opinion of my morals, passed her off as a legal spouse. Talking of her, he said, "she was the truest of women"—from which I immediately inferred she could *not* be his wife, and so it turned out.

March 20, 1814—Sparred with Jackson again yesterday morning, and shall tomorrow. I feel all the better for it, in spirits, though my arms and shoulders are very stiff from it. Mem. to attend the pugilistic dinner:—Marquess Huntley is in the chair.

April 9, 1814—I am but just returned to town, from which you may infer that I have been out of it; and I have been boxing, for exercise, with Jackson for this last month daily. I have also been drinking, and, on one occasion, with three other friends at the Cocoa Tree, from six till four, yea, unto five in the matin.

April 26, 1814—I can't for the head of me, add a line worth scribbling; my "vein" is quite gone, and my present occupations are of the gymnastic order—boxing and fencing—and my principal conversation is with my macaw and Bayle.

June 19, 1814—My mornings are late, and passed in fencing and box-
ing, and a variety of most unpoetical exercises, very wholesome, &c.,
but would be very disagreeable to my friends, whom I am obliged to
exclude during their operation.

September in the Bleachers

TOM CLARK

In the bathroom the bad dudes
are putting money on Ali & Kenny Norton
up & down the row of stalls
little coveys of guys with tiny radios
callin out the blow by blow:
Round two to Muhammad! Whoo!

I listen to all this while I'm pissing
& the national anthem's playing outside
then make it back up thru the hot dog line
to catch the first inning, grinning,
my heart tells me Vida will shut out Kansas City tonight

He goes right ahead & does it before my eyes.

Each Poem of Mine

DANIELA CRĂSNARU

Translated from the Romanian by Adam J. Sorkin and the poet

the ring where I'm down for the count
to your screams and taunts.

Passing

JIM DANIELS

In gym class boxing, Fat Feeney got paired
with Big Eddie Lavendar. Coach Wendler
circled the ring, taunted Feeney,
pushed him back when he tried to run.

Lavendar flattened Feeney's nose.
He wouldn't get up. Lay there frozen,
an iceberg waiting for arctic silence.
We filed past to the locker room
kicking him, spitting out all our names
for boys like him who wouldn't fight.

The High Dive: *A* for a dive. *C* for a jump.
F for sissies. Feeney climbed up, jiggling
layers of flesh. We wanted to see the splash.
Coach screamed *Jump Feeney jump!*
We chanted *Jump Feeney jump!*
Our voices echoed off tile, rang out
over still water. Feeney held the rail.
His tears fell to the board. We waited, screaming,
bare-assed on the benches.
When he climbed down, Wendler paddled him.
In the locker room, our arms popped out,
punched him between the rows.

Doug Molinski stomped on Feeney's face
in the parking lot. Everyone knew
he never fought back. A punching bag
for anyone's random black-and-blue anger.

Molinski wouldn't stop because,
because, who knows. Feeney's face
a bloody mess surgery couldn't fix.

Coach used to yell
You're a big boy, Feeney,
hit somebody, as if those two things
went hand in hand. Molinski back in a year.
Feeney's mother took him away—who knows where.
You know how dogs can sniff out fear?
Yeah, I punched him a few times:
jab, jab. jab. I took my *C.*

Moorer Denies Holyfield in Twelve

OLENA KALYTIAK DAVIS

Caesar's Palace.
The way life keeps splitting itself in two.

Twenty four hours later Florida
had pushed itself under
the wheels of our white Olds.
My father getting out
of the car. I'm squinting, his
shirt is that bright.

I was stunned for a minute
but was able to clear my head.

I'm on the phone now, trying to keep this front
from moving over his white cloud of a head,
because my father used to be two men,
but now he's old.

One minute you're talking weather. Then,
a nasty left-right in the second round.

I didn't mean to start talking obstacles, hooks,
        comebacks.
But, suddenly, I'm going down saying:

I've been holding on with my teeth.
I've developed this strange social stutter.

I had to let my cutman go.

Everywhere the Pacific

WAYNE DODD

Jesus Christ I used to watch
Carl "Bobo" Olson in Honolulu,
fighting his way up against
middleweights and even an occasional
light heavy from the mainland
on his way back down
to the tank, and it was sweet
to see him.
          Outside the gym
the nights were heavy
with their tropic air
of promise, and sailors schooled
through the streets incessantly
hungry
        for the moment.
Out Kalakaua Boulevard the beaches
were already beginning to
melt down into gold bars
and hotels in California.
           There
in the gym we sweated,
fairskinned and tough
to land a clean shot on, tattooed
inside our heads and chests
with the rich prowl of scenes
from our own lives.
          Somewhere,
in a warm dark the blood
pumps perfect through, I
wade into lush grass beyond
the overhead reach
of a tree, my moist hand trembling
in hers, the sound of insects

a membrane inside my skull.
We bob and duck
under branches tipped with color
we cannot see. This,
we always know, is the big one
and ply both hands furiously
to the body.
     Meanwhile,
everywhere the Pacific
continues its long wash of salt
over whatever it touches.

Boxing

PAGE DOUGHERTY

1. ATTIC ON 34TH STREET
My brothers never boxed,
not with gloves and helmets in a fair ring,
nothing organized or sporting.
They sparred with words and tense
bouts of fear, angry at they knew not what,
the rules eluding them, everything about them
flailing as they spun vocabulary without target,
at times fist-hurling at each other the newly
found tongue, first *bastard,* with its sting
of misbelonging, then bolder: *fuck you, little shit.*
Turd breath, with all the dun and longing
born from casting out into nothing—
shared space, shared beams of sunlight
bending into the just-rented house,
its 19th century rafters smacking their heads.
They butterflied above it all, a mother's
work life, her one-pillow bed, feigning manliness,
slugging away, one gaining, then the other,
pummeling sadness in the airless lodes.

2. EARTH
My husband spars at a mine entrance
after three dayshift guys throw down
our leaflets and curl around us.
Where the 2 × 4 comes from is not clear,
or who first raises it in true ire.

Once my husband yelled on a picket line
"give me an M 16," as if to Vietnam
those Jersey City cops, that he might Cu Chi them
into submission, evoking the rifle which
after 6 months into his tour, he'd put down,

but only ended up that night in Kearney's jail,
my soon-to-be betrothed. My role—
consecutive meetings, hours phoning lawyers.

Now we're in the mud and red-dog bits,
miles up a road along an absurd
mine-ravaged often errant creek.
Again it is us against them, their swelling
number, the lot of us, some women
among the men. Then the weapon
of wood, held now by one of theirs,
grabbed by my husband, who drops it
to go at it man to man, to raise his dukes
like twigs, all this quick-time, jabs
the other miner in his head, K.O.s him.

Three timely cars of state police
to bust us, less polite than other times
to us women, *where you from,*
fists bedding their palms.
But clearly, we won the fight,
the man just now raising himself up,
brushing off the muck, spitting to the earth
that did not render him strength or insight,
only enough venom to chuck our fliers
about miners coming together into the creek,
and *just wait buddy, I know where you work,*
we women erased by the rage of men,
and borne away in the back of police cars.

3. GIFTS
My husband buys our son boxing gear
one Christmas when we can't think
what to give. He's met bullies
on the street who grabbed a hat,
ripped off a bus pass, and once a tough
rose from the safe zone of comrades
to wag a small knife. Our boy's learned to run,
shows good timing, and waits for height

to free him from the victim years.
Two pairs of leather gloves
with velcro flaps, leather ear-guards
to save bone-hard skull and all its ragged contents.
My son swings wildly, without skill
or rage or much intent.
He knows his duty, a few afternoons
of smacking leathery weight against
his father's growing gut, reaching for the shoulders
that raised him through stores, up slag and limestone rocks,
the ridiculous and sublimes of a powerful love.
Now they're set to sock each other,
and this goes on until the new year's mercy.

They live, quite passively, inside the drawer,
partner to the growing pile of caps
with every sports team's name machine-stitched
across the front and the secret stash
of naked-girl magazines I come upon
when searching for my lost black sweater,
& I realize it's the laundry that always
steals something, you must wait and it will
find you. It is different, how
we conceal what is only half-way ours,
or what we never asked for.

4. INCORPORATION
How women have studied men, the flip
of the jaw upward, defiant and sultry,
the right to leer,
the dance, the jab and punch, the high five,
the femur, the wild embrace.
Rib stance, exhale, the x-muscle tensed,
the forgetting of breasts
or vagina until one is all outward strength,
all sinew and rehearsal,
a fist-garnered silence, a protected mouth.

Bendy's Sermon

SIR ARTHUR CONAN DOYLE

Bendigo, the well-known Nottingham prize-fighter, became converted to
religion and preached at revival meetings throughout the country.

You didn't know of Bendigo! Well, that knocks me out!
Who's your board school teacher? What's he been about?
Chock-a-block with fairy-tales—full of useless cram,
And never heard o' Bendigo, the pride of Nottingham!

Bendy's short for Bendigo. You should see him peel!
Half of him was whalebone, half of him was steel,
Fightin' weight eleven ten, five foot nine in height,
Always ready to oblige if you want a fight.

I could talk of Bendigo from here to kingdom come,
I guess before I ended you would wish your dad was dumb,
I'd tell you how he fought Ben Caunt, and how the Deaf 'un fell,
But the game is done, and the men are gone—and maybe it's as well.

Bendy he turned Methodist—he said he felt a call,
He stumped the country preachin' and you bet he filled the hall,
If you see him in the pulpit, a'bleatin' like a lamb,
You'd never know bold Bendigo, the pride of Nottingham.

His hat was like a funeral, he'd got a waiter's coat,
With a hallelujah collar and a choker round his throat,
His pals would laugh and say in chaff that Bendigo was right
In takin' on the devil, since he'd no one else to fight.

But he was very earnest, improvin' day by day,
A-workin' and a-preachin' just as his duty lay,
But the devil he was waitin', and in the final bout
He hit him hard below his guard and knocked poor Bendy out.

Now I'll tell you how it happened. He was a preachin' down at
    Brum,
He was billed just like a circus, you should see the people come,
The chapel it was crowded, and in the foremost row
There was half a dozen bruisers who'd a grudge at Bendigo.

There was Tommy Platt of Bradford, Solly Jones of Perry Bar,
Long Connor from the Bull Ring, the same wot drew with Carr,
Jack Ball the fightin' gunsmith, Joe Murphy from the Mews,
And Iky Moss, the bettin' boss, the Champion of the Jews.

A very pretty handful a-sittin' in a string,
Full of beer and impudence, ripe for anything,
Sittin' in a string there, right under Bendy's nose,
If his message was for sinners, he could make a start on those.

Soon he heard them chaffin': 'Hi, Bendy! Here's a go!'
'How much are you coppin' by this Jump to Glory show?'
'Stow it Bendy! Left the ring! Mighty spry of you!
Didn't everybody know the ring was leavin' you?'

Bendy fairly sweated as he stood above and prayed,
'Look down, O Lord, and grip me with a strangle hold!' he said.
'Fix me with a strangle hold! Put a stop on me!
I'm slippin', Lord, I'm slippin' and I'm clingin' hard to Thee!'

But the roughs they kept on chaffin' and the uproar it was such
That the preacher in the pulpit might be talkin' double Dutch,
Till a workin' man he shouted out, a-jumpin' to his feet,
'Give us a lead, your reverence, and heave 'em in the street.'

Then Bendy said, 'Good Lord, since first I left my sinful ways,
Thou knowest that to Thee alone I've given up my days,
But now, dear Lord'—and here he laid his Bible on the shelf—
'I'll take with your permission, just five minutes for myself.'

He vaulted from the pulpit like a tiger from a den,
They said it was a lovely sight to see him floor his men;

Right and left, and left and right, straight and true and hard,
Till the Ebenezer Chapel looked more like a knacker's yard.

Platt was standin' on his back and lookin' at his toes,
Solly Jones of Perry Bar was feelin' for his nose,
Connor of the Bull Ring had all that he could do
Rakin' for his ivories that lay about the pew.

Jack Ball the fightin' gunsmith was in a peaceful sleep,
Joe Murphy lay across him, all tied up in a heap,
Five of them was twisted in a tangle on the floor,
And Iky Moss, the bettin' boss, had sprinted for the door.

Five repentant fightin' men, sitting in a row,
Listenin' to words of grace from Mister Bendigo,
Listenin' to his reverence—all as good as gold,
Pretty little baa-lambs, gathered to the fold.

So that's the way that Bendy ran his mission in the slum,
And preached the Holy Gospel to the fightin' men of Brum,
'The Lord,' said he, 'has given me His message from on high,
And if you interrupt Him, I will know the reason why.'

But to think of all your schoolin', clean wasted, thrown away,
Darned if I can make out what you're learnin' all the day,
Grubbin' up old fairy-tales, fillin' up with cram,
And didn't know of Bendigo, the pride of Nottingham!

Boxing Towards My Birth

JACK DRISCOLL

My mother wanted to name me after an Irish thinker:
James Joyce, Sean O'Casey, William Butler Yeats.
But my father thought better of Jack Dempsey,
the "Manassa Mauler." I grew up
shadowboxing with the famous dead.

In the kitchen
my mother read me sad poems that danced for pages
while my father drank himself into the Friday night fights.
Between rounds he stumbled in for bottles of beer,
threw jabs so close to my face
I could feel my first teeth beginning to bleed.
At five I knew words like "knockout," "low blow," "straight right."
       That Christmas
I found red boxing gloves under the tree.
They each reminded me of a reindeer's heart
laced tightly around my skinny wrists.
Half naked,
I stood in front of the full length mirror.
My father, smiling, made the sound of a bell
and pushed me closer to the thick glass,
towards the anger of that first punch
I aimed so willingly at myself.

Pornography

JOSEPH DUEMER

Combien qu'il soit rudement fait
La matiere est si tres notable
Qu'elle amende tout le mesfait.
—Villon

The body is the instrument on which imagination plays.
The temple prostitute sent by the king to seduce & civilize
Enkidu brought her guitar along, as well as her makeup kit.
She sang him away from the animals & taught him language
by whispering songs into his sunburned ears that rang
with sympathetic chords. Thus he forgot his nature & world.

Ask King Gilgamesh—the truest friend is the wild man who
has just begun to master the vocabularies of the city
& still dreams the live & flickering savanna hot with sun, blood
staining the grass where a lion has killed a zebra, flies. Peace.
Resting in the shade as the sun passes the ferocious zenith.
His memories give him strength the king can bend to use.

Well-practiced, she took his hand & smoothed it with her own.
The city flourishes upon sophisticated grammars, but sometimes
a gesture goes so deep we feel it like a breath, or song
that drifts from a smoky alley recalling low hills flickering
under sun, blood. Or late at night two people without reason flare
matchlight into each other's eyes & reach out their hands toward . . .

Impossible now to recover that which once they were
before the gesture. The body live with animal faith is the instrument
on which imagination plays. Someone lowers the radio to a whisper
& flicks on the lobby television in an SRO hotel. The old men
scratch their beards & settle on a greasy couch, blowing smoke.
Two fighters are entering the ring, white beneath the klieg lights;

on-screen colors flicker in & out of register revealing the three souls
of each man—vegetal, animal & rational. The referee dances
across the ring, a ghostly figure in charge of making beauty out
of violence. Next door, the movies are threaded into the projectors
at the Apple Theater, an old garage perched above an on-ramp where
the grungy carpets & scarlet velvet curtains muffle the footsteps

of the patrons, but not the sanctified shrieks of the actresses who
fuck the audience with light. The beefy lips of their vaginas are
    swollen
as the gash above one fighter's eye, who is peering through a mist
of blood for his opponent's face, an image of the truth collecting
on the cerebral cortex at the back of his shaken brain. The king
smashes his fist like a hammer into the jaw of the wild man

from the steppe, who does not crumble but strikes a ferocious blow
to the king's belly that makes him shit blood on the ground.
Cracking the curbs, they fight forty days & nights outside the tavern
where posters advertise LIVE NUDE GIRLS nipples & pubic hair
obliterated by a cold black bar. They fall into each other's arms.
Thus is born the psyche of Western Man—a brawl outside a bar

at the beginning of history. From this beginning, a short step
leads to fear of death & terror in the face of women. In the movies
they are slugging it out to an endless loop of bass guitar.
The rhetoric of literature since the ancients admits sexual desire
as well as its twin politics: Aphrodite & Ares strung up in Hephestos'
cunning net—Homer's dirty joke in the form of an aside

after the women (every one a queen or princess) have gone to bed
& only the slave girls dark & sinuous as the Nile & half naked
in the heat are still up dozing in the shadowed corners of the room—
their imperishable desire a melody that persists through history,
modal & efficient, turning up under different titles. Aficionados
watch to see if the champion has broken a sweat by the time

he enters the ring. Sweat equals desire & readiness, salt & sweet.
There are pheromones to perpetuate the species & others designed

specifically by the gods to break your heart. Didn't you know?
The old gods live in the chaotic interstices of natural
        selection, ever
& anon creating the world. That's *his* territory, the culture hero
Dick-for-Brains. Usually portrayed iconographically as a *roué*,

the noun derived from the past participle of the old French word
for *breaking on the wheel*. A sport, a wolf (in outdated jive), some
poor doofus who, having failed again, is driving that stretch of
        highway
between 2:00 A.M. & dawn angry as hell & all its angels who will
again be falling drunk & disappointed into bed because he is a man
who deserves his fate, unable in every account to turn irony

upon experience. Not one of the heroes, he will do anything
for love. The old men are disappointed because the fighters have
battered each other to a draw. No money changes hands. They
can hear the crunch of gravel as the patrons next door pull out
of the parking lot & glide around the corner, their tail lights
smeared like blood on the pavement wet with increasing rain.

On Hurricane Jackson

ALAN DUGAN

Now his nose's bridge is broken, one eye
will not focus and the other is a stray;
trainers whisper in his mouth while one ear
listens to itself, clenched like a fist;
generally shadowboxing in a smoky room,
his mind hides like the aching boys
who lost a contest in the Panhellenic games
and had to take the back roads home,
but someone else, his perfect youth,
laureled in newsprint and dollar bills,
triumphs forever on the great white way
to the statistical Sparta of the champs.

My Father's Fights

STUART DYBEK

His best
were the two
between Chuck Davey
& Chico Vejar:

Davey, balding,
insurance man
in trunks
with a jab
precise as a surgeon;

Vejar, Latin legs,
legs from where
they grow up playing soccer,
that don't fold,
his own blood
shiny on his gloves;

My father,
in the stuffed chair
facing the Zenith,
throwing so many punches
no one could
get near.

Hurricane

BOB DYLAN AND JACQUES LEVY

Pistol shots ring out in the barroom night
Enter Patty Valentine from the upper hall
She sees the bartender in a pool of blood
Cries out, "My God, they killed them all!"
Here comes the story of the Hurricane
The man the authorities came to blame
For somethin' that he never done
Put in a prison cell, but one time he coulda been
The champion of the world.

Three bodies lyin' there does Patty see
And another man named Bello, movin' around mysteriously
"I didn't do it," he says, and he throws up his hands
"I was only robbin' the register, I hope you understand
I saw them leavin'," he says, and he stops
"One of us had better call up the cops"
And so Patty calls the cops
And they arrive on the scene with their red lights flashin'
In the hot New Jersey night

Meanwhile, far away in another part of town
Rubin Carter and a couple of friends are drivin' around
Number one contender for the middleweight crown
Had no idea what kinda shit was about to go down
When a cop pulled him over to the side of the road
Just like the time before and the time before that
In Paterson that's just the way things go
If you're black you might as well not show up on the street
'Less you wanta draw the heat

Alfred Bello had a partner and he had a rap for the cops
Him and Arthur Dexter Bradley were just out prowlin' around

He said, "I saw two men runnin' out, they looked like
        middleweights
They jumped into a white car with out-of-state plates"
And Miss Patty Valentine just nodded her head
Cop said, "Wait a minute boys, this one's not dead"
So they took him to the infirmary
And though this man could hardly see
They told him that he could identify the guilty men

Four in the mornin' and they haul Rubin in
Take him to the hospital and they bring him upstairs
The wounded man looks up through his one dyin' eye
Says, "Wha'd you bring him in here for? He ain' the guy!"
Yes, here's the story of the Hurricane
The man the authorities came to blame
For somethin' that he never done
Put in a prison cell, but one time he coulda been
The champion of the world

Four months later, the ghettoes are in flame
Rubin's in South America, fightin' for his name
While Arthur Dexter Bradley's still in the robbery game
And the cops are puttin' the screws to him, lookin' for somebody to
        blame
"Remember that murder that happened in a bar?"
"Remember you said you saw the getaway car?"
"You think you'd like to play ball with the law?"
"Think it mighta been that fighter that you saw runnin' that night?"
"Don't forget that you are white"

Arthur Dexter Bradley said, "I'm really not sure"
Cops said, "A poor boy like you could use a break
We got you for the motel job and we're talkin' to your friend Bello
Now you don't wanta have to go back to jail, be a nice fellow
You'll be doin' society a favor
That sonofabitch is brave and gettin' braver
We want to put his ass in stir

We want to pin this triple murder on him
He ain't no Gentleman Jim"

Rubin could take a man out with just one punch
But he never did like to talk about it all that much
It's my work, he'd say, and I do it for pay
And when it's over I'd just as soon go on my way
Up to some paradise
Where the trout streams flow and the air is nice
And ride a horse along a trail
But then they took him to the jail house
Where they try to turn a man into a mouse

All of Rubin's cards were marked in advance
That trial was a pig-circus, he never had a chance
The judge made Rubin's witnesses drunkards from the slums
To the white folks who watched he was a revolutionary bum
And to the black folks he was just a crazy nigger
No one doubted that he pulled the trigger
And though they could not produce the gun
The D.A. said he was the one who did the deed
And the all-white jury agreed

Rubin Carter was falsely tried
The crime was murder "one", guess who testified?
Bello and Bradley and they both baldly lied
And the newspapers, they all went along for the ride
How can the life of such a man
Be in the palm of some fool's hand?
To see him obviously framed
Couldn't help but make me feel ashamed to live in a land
Where justice is a game

Now all the criminals in their coats and their ties
Are free to drink martinis and watch the sun rise
While Rubin sits like Buddha in a ten-foot cell
An innocent man in a living hell
That's the story of the Hurricane

But it won't be over till they clear his name
And give him back the time he's done
Put in a prison cell, but one time he coulda been
The champion of the world

Jack Johnson Does the Eagle Rock

CORNELIUS EADY

Perhaps he left the newspaper stand that morning
    dazed, a few pennies lighter,
The illustration of the crippled ocean liner
    with the berth he had the money
But not the skin to buy
Engraving itself
On that portion of the mind reserved for
    lucky breaks.
Perhaps the newsboy, a figure too small to
    bring back,
Actually heard his laugh,
As the *S.S. Titanic,* sans one prize fighter,
Goes down again all over New York,
Watched his body dance
As his arms lift the ship, now a simple millimeter thick,
    above his head
In the bustling air, lift it up
As though it was meant to happen.

The Feats of Prime Jack Randall, O!

PIERCE EGAN

dedicated to Dan Donnelly, the Irish champion

'Tis of the ring, I mean to sing,
The feats of *prime* JACK RANDALL, O!
Young Pad *lywhack,* has got the *nack,*
In *row,* a *mill,* or a *turn-up,* O!
'Twas BELCHER's name, and DUTCH SAM's fame,
And CRIB's manhood he did revere,
That caus'd his heart to make a start,
Praises to gain both far and near;
At St. Gile's Pound, he *box'd* 'em round,
The PATS cried out—"See the darling, O!
He's got the *trick,* that makes 'em *sick*—
To be sure it is JACK RANDALL, O!"

> *Chorus:*
> Then fill your glass, and let it pass,
> Here's a health to "Young Paddy, O!"
> Who *floors* them all, both great and small,
> Does *finishing* JACK RANDALL O!

The *milling coves* came out in droves,
At *Shepperton* to see RANDALL, O!
With BELASCO fight, it was delight
To view the stile he won it, O!
The *Fancy Lads* upon their *prads,*
Loud cheering o this NONPAREIL!
Who *mills* so gay, and gets away,
Like merry dancing in a reel;
His *precious* hits, like terrible fits,
Doubling-up his opponents, O!
He gain'd the day, as if at play,
Did *finishing* JACK RANDALL, O!

His fame now rais'd, by ev'ry one prais'd,
Loud *chaunting* prime JACK RANDALL, O!
In various parts, the PATS' *warm* hearts
Swore he could beat a whole PARISH, O!
JACK took the lead, to shew his breed:
The WATERMAN, with *science* great,
Made many stops, got heavy *waps,*
Receiving too upon his *pate.*
Won battles EIGHT in easy state,
Payne, Levy, Holt, Dick, Dodd, Walton, O!
With NATURE's guide, JACK's only pride,
A natural boxer is RANDALL, O!

The Man Who Beat Hemingway

MARTÍN ESPADA

for Kermit Forbes, Key West, Florida, 1994

In 1937, Robert Johnson
still sang the Walking Blues,
the insistent churchbell of his guitar,
the moaning congregation of his voice,
a year before the strychnine flavored
his whiskey.

In the time of Robert Johnson,
you called yourself Battling Geech,
135 pounds, the ball of your bicep rolling
when you sickled the left hook
from a crouch, elbows blocking
hammers to the ribcage.
Florida for a Black man
was Robert Johnson, moaning:
the signs that would not feed you
hand-lettered in diner windows,
the motels that kept all beds white.

Here, in a ring rigged behind the mansion,
next to the first swimming pool
in Key West, you sparred with Hemingway.
He was 260 pounds in 1937, thick arms
lunging for you, so you slid crablike
beneath him, your shaven head
spotlit with sweat against his chest.
Only once did his leather fist tumble you,
sprawling across canvas
white as sun.

Now, nearing eighty, one eye stolen
from the socket, one gold tooth

anchored to your jaw,
you awoke this morning
and weighed the hurricane-heavy air
of Key West in your fighter's hands,
three decades after Papa Hemingway
choked himself with a shotgun.
You should stand before the mansion
on Whitehead Street, telling the amazed tourists
that you are the man who beat Hemingway,
and it happened here,
even if the plaque
leaves out your name.

Bus Depot Reunion

DAVID ALLAN EVANS

Just over the edge
of my *Life* a young sailor
bounds from a Greyhound's
hiss into his mother's hug,
steps back, trades hands
with his father, then turns
to an old, hunched man
maybe his grandfather—

no hand, no word goes out,
they regard each other,

waiting for something, and
now their hands cup,

they begin to crouch
and spar, the old man

coming on like a pro,
snuffling, weaving,

circling, flicks
out a hook like a lizard's tongue,

the boy ducking, countering,
moving with his moves,

biffing at the bobbing
yellow grin, the clever

head, never landing a real
punch, never taking one

until suddenly, exactly
together they quit,

throw an arm around each other
and walk away laughing

Shadow Boxer

DAVID EVANS JR.

Always move.
Dance in the light,
in the smoke.

Keep your guard.
Work the jab.
Stick and move.

Counter.
They're all watching.
All listening.

Uppercut, left hook.
Straight right.
Never die.

I can win
my way out—
hammer through it all.

Look at the speed,
the blurring speed.
Look at the cool head—

the head of that shadow
weaving on the wall.
Listen to it.
Listen.

Fists

RICHARD FOERSTER

Photo of my father as a boxer, ca. 1929

Ah, the impenetrable knot.
How the radiant star
of each hand has collapsed
to a brown core. Snub-
nosed mambas long
as his arms. Surrogate cocks,
his cowries, his charms. Shrunken
skulls with lips and eyes
sewn fast. How mute
yet mocking, these amputees
swaggering their bald huzzahs

before the world. I'm twice
what he was there, the stunning
gesture punctuating
the decades before my birth,
the blue contusion back—
lighting my sisters' Bronx,
then mine. Punch, parry,
counterpunch—he's
dead—yet still these clenched
fists, these mallets gaveling
against the planks of heaven.

Boxing

RICHARD FROST

Couldn't afford not to, my friends
insisting: with my long reach
I should jab well enough to unbalance
and uppercut any son of a bitch.

Nested deep in memory,
the setup, first day of drill,
and fat Vern, reportedly slow,
coming out in a mayhem of leather.

Wait a minute! I yell, and he doesn't.
Then, at my locker, I button
my jacket atop my blue gymshorts
and reel out without taking a shower.

Famous at home, I watch boxing
all I'm able. Nothing gets past me—
no cutmen, no refs, no judges.
Long years, I tell—*Long years I was in there.*

Champ Joe Louis

"LITTLE BILL" GAITHER

I came all the way from Chicago to see Joe Louis
    and Max Schmeling fight
I came all the way from Chicago to see Joe Louis
    and Max Schmeling fight
Schmeling went down like the Titanic
    when Joe gave him just one hard right

Well, you've heard of the King of Swing, well Joe is
    the King of Gloves
Well, you've heard of the King of Swing, well Joe is
    the King of Gloves
Now he's the World Heavyweight Champion,
    a man that this whole world loves

It was only two minutes and four seconds poor Schmeling
    was down on his knees
It was only two minutes and four seconds poor Schmeling
    was down on his knees
He looked like he was praying to the Good Lord
    to "Have mercy on me, please!"

If I'd had a million dollars would have bet every dime on Joe
If I'd had a million dollars would have bet every dime on Joe
I'd've been a rich man this very day
    and I wouldn't have to worry no more

A Fighter Learns of Hands

CHARLES GHIGNA

Hands were not made for hitting.
Learn this and you will know much about hands.
Trace the lines of life in your palm,
Search beyond skin to the constellation of bone
Where the truth about hands is hidden.
Take them outside for a walk
And unglove them in the snow.
Watch them shape the chill air as you
Reach to capture and hold your white breathing.
Close your eyes and place their fingertips
Along the parting of your lips.
Cup them gently against your ears like muffs
And listen to their silence.
You are learning the meaning of hands.

But if in some heated future you forget
And must use them instead for battle,
Must make them into fists and send them against another,
Learn first to fear the hands that hold no memory.
Treat them with suspicion, tape them tighter than a wound
And hide them like a broken secret deep into leather.
Keep the left one near the corner of your eye,
Cock the right one like a cobra at your chin.
Let it strike above the ring. Let it paint the canvas red
Until the final bell lulls you to sleep like a child
Dreaming of stars, until those stars are in your hands,
Until your hands are awake, and beating.

Dempsey, Dempsey

HORACE GREGORY

Everybody give the big boy a hand,
a big hand for the big boy, Dempsey,
failure king of the U.S.A.

Maybe the big boy's coming back,
there's a million boys that want to come back
with hell in their eyes and a terrible sock
that almost connects.
They've got to come back, out of the street,
out of some lowdown, lousy job
or take a count with Dempsey.

When he's on his knees for a count
and a million dollars cold,
a million boys go down with him
yelling:
             Hit him again Dempsey,
kill him for me Dempsey,
Christ sake Dempsey,
my God they're killing Dempsey,
it's Dempsey down, Dempsey, Dempsey.

The million men and a million boys,
come out of hell and crawling back,
maybe they don't know what they're saying,
maybe they don't dare
but they know what they mean:
Knock down the big boss,
o, my little Dempsey,
my beautiful Dempsey
with that God in heaven smile
and quick, god's body leaping,
not afraid, leaping, rising—

hit him again, he cut my pay check, Dempsey.
My God, Dempsey's down—
he cut my pay check—
Dempsey's down, down,
the bastards are killing Dempsey.
Listen, they made me go to war
and somebody did something wrong to my wife
while I was gone.
Hit him again Dempsey, don't be a quitter
like I am Dempsey,
o, for Jesus Christ, I'm out.
I can't get up, I'm dead, my legs
are dead, see, I'm no good,
they got me and I'm out,
down for the count.
I've quit, quit again,
only God save Dempsey, make him get up again,
Dempsey, Dempsey

British Lads and Black Millers

BOB GREGSON

You gentlemen of fortune attend unto my ditty,
    A few lines I have penn'd upon this great fight,
In the centre of England the noble place is pitched on,
    For the Valour of this Country, or America's delight:
    The sturdy black doth swear,
    The moment he gets there,
    The planks the stage is built on, he'll make them blaze and
        smoke;
    Then Cribb, with smiling face,
    Says, these boards, I'll ne'er disgrace;
They're relations of mine, they're Old English oak.
Brave Molineaux replied, I've never been denied
    To fight the foes of Britain on such planks as those:
If relationship you claim, bye-and-bye you'll know my name:
    I'm the swellish, milling cove that can drub my foes.
    The Cribb replied with haste,
    You slave, I will you baste,
As your Master us'd to cane you, 'twill bring things to your mind,
    If from bondage you've got clear,
    To impose on Britons here,
You'd better stopp'd with Christophe, you'll quickly find.
The garden of freedom is the British land we live in,
    And welcomes every slave from his banish'd isle;
Allows them to impose on a nation good and generous,
    To incumber and pollute our native soil;
    But John Bull cries out aloud,
    We're neither poor nor proud,
But open to all nations, let them come from where they will.
    The British lads that's here,
    Quite strangers are to fear:
Here's Tom Cribb, with bumpers round, for he can them mill.

Fighting

DONALD HALL

Your left foot moves, and my
right hand raises
itself to block your fist, while my left
jabs at your unprotected
jaw. But as I touch you I
wobble to my knees. Dear old
sparrer, we knock
each other out.

Buck

MICHAEL S. HARPER

I owe him for pictures
of champions I'd known,
or never seen,
or never known
and seen as men like
him, arched now
on a drunk
to ease arthritis,
his red tie
soaked in vomit,
his blue-ringed eyes
etched in glaucoma,
menace in serge-body
on his day off
near the cubicle
where he polishes
shoes, downtown
handballers at this Y.

Tomorrow
he will kneel
over the soft leather
of his polished nails,
his glasses pouched
as two black circles,
past years at sea,
his prison blindness,
concessions lost
to three promoters
the night Joe Louis
broke in the garden;
that he could box Sugar
in his prime,

hit like Archie,
teach Gavilan to bolo,
all this in signed
photos of his gallery,
is his hangover and cure
of the future of brushes.

Four bits,
he's changed men into boys
when they ask of his photos,
black and greased
in red velvet,
buckdancing in high-topped shoes,
he'll tell a lawyer
his two cushions
are his hero chamber;
'even with glasses off
I can tell you're a boy.'
He'll speak of his father
in Panama, lost and broken
in the canal
where ships cruise
to Frisco
keelhauling his shadow,
how he followed
his known sister
who'd died ironing
his suit cleaned
on her kitchen benches.

When my third son
died in intensive,
after early birth,
he took two photos
of his champions
for two sons I'd lost,
and signed their backs;
patting my shoulder

with mahogany nails
he called them grandsons,
turned toward two men
with black, unlaced shoes
patting their sleeping soles.

Homage to the Brown Bomber

MICHAEL S. HARPER

Speed of the punch,
its dancing, rhythmic fluency
in short space, short duration,
its honing light of the Garden,
the Stadium: each gladiator falls
to be redeemed in porcelain speech,
however simple, never glib,
the nation's devastation
coming home to roost.

Born near sacred Indian mounds in Alabama,
broken in the "destroy" kitchens
of Chevrolet and Cadillac,
short tours at Comiskey Park,
the heavy bag the strange fruit
of commerce, newsprint,
without the dazzling photographs
of Sonja Henie's pirouettes
at the Olympic Games,
in shared bedrooms, horns
plenty for the unprotected.

Sugar dazzled too,
but the brute poetry
of the finisher,
how to wait on hidden impulse
of a bannered song,
that was ammunition
for the lost struggle
of the chaingang,
of the limousine.

Taps at Vegas,
new shrubbery

at Arlington,
grist for radio, the stooped flares
of camels
on deserts of yesterdays,
bright lungs blanching tomorrows,
barrows at rest.

Free Fantasia: Tiger Flowers

ROBERT HAYDEN

for Michael

The sporting people
along St. Antoine—
that scufflers'
paradise of ironies—
    bet salty money
on his righteous
    hook and jab.

I was a boy then, running
(unbeknownst to Pa)
errands for Miss Jackie
and Stack-o'-Diamonds' Eula Mae.
    . . . Their perfumes,
rouged Egyptian faces.
    Their pianolas jazzing.

O Creole babies,
Dixie odalisques,
speeding through cutglass
dark to see the macho angel
    trick you'd never
turn, his bluesteel prowess
    in the ring.

Hardshell believers
amen'd the wreck
as God A'mighty's
will. I'd thought
    such gaiety could not
die. Nor could our
    elegant avenger.

The Virgin Forest
by Rousseau—
its psychedelic flowers
towering, its deathless
    dark dream figure
death the leopard
    claws—I choose it
now as elegy
    for Tiger Flowers.

A Ballad of the Life and Times of Joe Louis
The Great Brown Bomber

CALVIN HERNTON

I.

Know I must and think I will
Sound the gong and make a song of shimmering steel
And make it real
For the Great Brown Bomber born on the Buckalow Mountains
    among the Alabama Hills!

Lesser men
    who raving
    who babble senility
    who name lakes after themselves who eyes glint
    who lips twitch
Are not abandon to shipwreck cold and naked shock
    but are
    paraded before the world
    and live in mansions
If not in peace.

So come and go
Ye throngs of thousands, ye mermaids of cognition
Hail! Hail! Hail!
Come and go back to fireside chats and the gospel songs
    of the Golden Gate Quartet.
Come and go
    when I was a boy down in Chattanooga Tennessee
    when black folks congregate in Big Mable's bootlegged
    liquor joint
    and children hovered outside against the storefront
    windows painted black all the way up to the heights of our
    wool-laden heads
    when the entire ghetto street grew quiet
    in open daylight
    when pride quelled beating hearts still

and over the only wireless in the neighborhood
we stood as though around a throne
And all ears awaited the sound of the gong.

II.
Hail! Hail! Hail!

JUNE 22ND 1938

YANKEE STADIUM

ROUND ONE

LOUIS COMES OUT MAKING A WINDING MOTION WITH HIS RIGHT
FOREARM

Just like the first time

AND HE SENDS A RIGHT TO SCHMELING'S JAW THAT STAGGERS
THE BIG GERMAN

NOW LOUIS SENDS ANOTHER, A THIRD, A FOURTH, ALL HITTERS!

And unlike the first time

LOUIS DOES NOT DROP HIS GUARD AFTER HITTING THE GERMAN
UNLIKE THE FIRST TIME

NOW SCHMELING TRIES TO COUNTER WITH A FUSILLADE OF
RIPPING RIGHTS AND LEFTS

BUT JOE JERKS BACK

SCHMELING BORES IN AND TOUCHES A LIGHT ONE LOUIS
        IGNORES IT

NOW THEN BUT LOUIS SMASHES HOME A RIGHT THAT SHOULD
HAVE DENTED CONCRETE DENTED CONCRETE DENTED CONCRETE!

And the nation exploded: "Beat That German, Brown Bomber,
    Beat That German!"
As if to himself the crippled man in the White House in the fireside
    chair murmured: "Beat The Nazi, Beat Him For The Morale Of
    The American Democracy!"
And in big Mabel's bootlegged liquor joint up and down the street
    everywhere shouted to the sky: "Whop Him, Joe, Baby, Whop
    Him For The Sake Of Colored Folks All Over Dhis Forsaken
    Land!"

WHEELING SCHMELING FACE FRONT TO THE ROPES JOE LOUIS
SENDS A VICIOUS RIGHT TO THE KIDNEY

Why does the announcer call Joe's punch "Vicious"?
Were it the other way around . . .

    A VICIOUS RIGHT TO THE KIDNEY VICIOUS TO THE KIDNEY AND
    SCHMELING SCREAMS LADIES AND GENTLEMEN
    SCREAMS IN PAIN PAIN PAIN WHEELING SCHMELING FACE FRONT
    TO THE ROPES OH MY COUNTRY ROPES OF THEE BLACK NECKS
        HANGING
    FROM THE POPLAR TREES MY COUNTRY TEARS OH VICIOUS RIGHT
    TO THE KIDNEY AND THE GERMAN BLOND SCREAMS IN AGONY
    ONE OF THE MOST TERRIFYING SOUNDS HEARD IN THE RING
LADIES AND GENTLEMEN
In the first round of the first fight when the Brown Bomber entered
    the ring and took off his robe
    there was another scream sounded the same
    hysterical scream from a WOMAN at ringside:
EEEEEEEEEEEOOOOOOOOOOOOOOOOOOOWWWWWWWWWWW
WHATS THAT HE GOT IN HIS PANTS OH GOD WHATS THAT BIG BULGING
IN HIS JOCKSTRAP

The Most Terrifying Sound Ever Heard In The Ring!

    MAX SCHMELING STRUGGLES TO LIFT HIS RIGHT ARM TO GRAB
    THE SIDE THE RIB THE GOOD OLD BAR B QED RIB BUT MAX IS
    PARALYZED PARALYZED
    REFEREE ARTHUR DONOVAN STEPS BETWEEN LOUIS AND THE
        GERMAN
    AND THE BROWN BOMBER IS POISING ANOTHER BOMB
Get *Away, Joe!* screams Referee Donovan
    LOUIS BLINKS AND BACKS AWAY GLARING ANGRILY AT THE
    WRITHING GERMAN . . . *scenes of flashing back images montage*
    what a ball of cotton with a great dictator mustache walking
    arrogantly from the olympic stands vowing he's never recognize
    no black coon even if he were the fastest man alive! . . . PEOPLE
    YELL FOR THE COUNT START THE COUNT THE COUNT BUT NO
    COUNT BEGINS MAX IS UTTERLY HELPLESS AND BUT FOR THE ROPES
    HE WOULD BE FLOPPED ALREADY HIS BLOND HEAD IS ROLLING
    LIKE RUBBER NOW THEN LOUIS HITS HIM WITH A SWISHING HOOK
    WITH A RIFLE TWIST TO IT SCHMELING DROPS BUT BEHOLD

STAGGERS UP ON KNOCKING KNEES WITHOUT TAKING A SINGLE
COUNT WOO WOO WOO THE GERMAN MUST REALLY BE SUPERMAN
NOW THEN BUT LOUIS AGAIN FLOORS THE GERM . . . SOMETHING
WHITE AN ILLEGAL TOWEL HAS BEEN THROWN INTO THE RING
FROM SCHMELING'S CORNER THE REFEREE IS THROWING THE
TOWEL BACK OUT OF THE RING . . . BUT SCHMELING HAS
CRUMPLED . . . FOR KEEPS . . . REFEREE DONOVAN BREASTROKES
WITH BOTH ARMS AND THE MASSACRE IS ENDED WHERE
SCHMELING WAKES UP IN THE HOSPITAL

Down in Chattanooga, Tennessee black men and women and
    children sang and wept and danced and prayed and rejoiced
And my grandmother said: "Lawd, childe, aint neber seed black folks
    be so proud, naw, not eben when ole Abraham Lincoln freed us
    aint neber seed black folks so hopeful, naw, not even when ole
Abe promised forty acres and one mule."
Hail! Hail! Oh, Hail!

    III.
I know I'm right and can't be wrong
Come along children and sang this song
And let it live
For the Great Brown Bomber born on the Buckalow Mountains
    among the Alabama Hills.

A pot of lye will sting and a bullet will kill
"Maw, I glad I win, I glad I win," quot the heavyweight champeen
O come along while the moon is shining bright
Gie me a pig feet and a bottle of gin
We gon raise the ruckus tonight!

IN EVERY MAIN BATTLE NO PERSON WHATEVER SHALL BE UPON THE
STAGE EXCEPT THE PRINCIPALS AND THEIR SECONDS: THE SAME
RULE TO BE OBSERVED IN THE BY-BATTLES, EXCEPT THAT IN THE
LATTER MR. BROUGHTON IS ALLOWED TO BE UPON THE STAGE TO
KEEP DECORUM AND TO ASSIST GENTLEMEN IN GETTING TO
THEIR PLACES THESE ARE MR. BROUGHTON'S RULES 1743

Fifty-nine heavyweight champeen fights fifty-one by knockout!
Flat feet stalker! Yo mamma wusnt no Mississippi delta queen
1619 nineteen African rattled their chains on the shores of
    Jamestown Virginia didn't come to America on no flower of
    May seeking no dream for

The white dream is a black nightmare.

ON THE MEN BEING STRIPPED IT SHALL BE THE DUTY OF THE
SECONDS TO EXAMINE THEIR DRAWERS, AND IF ANY OBJECTION
ARISES AS TO THE INSERTIN OF IMPROPER SUBSTANCES THEREIN
THEY SHALL APPEAL TO THEIR UMPIRES WHO WITH THE
CONCURRENCE OF THE REFEREE SHALL DIRECT WHAT
ALTERATIONS SHALL BE MADE THESE ARE LONDON PRIZE
RING RULES 1838 REVISED 1853

And a white woman screamed at ringside . . . *Here are the fruits for the*
    wind to suck and the buzzards to pluck
    seeds of ten thousand black men dripping blood
    from the magnolia tree . . .
STOPPING A FIGHT A MOMENT TOO SOON MAY BE UNFAIR TO
A GAME MAN: STOPPING IT A MOMENT TOO LATE MAY BE A TRAGEDY
SO SAITH ARTHUR DONOVAN

Runt fat men hallucinating jungle hunters, playing tough guys
Writing novels of wild life and statuesque imperialists
    with shotguns in their mouths
Jack London switching alongside the stout black legs of Jack Johnson
Burnt-out Hebrew novelist jerking off his dukes at the bicep pistons
    of the baddest black man ever to leap out of the criminology
        books
Who fought his way from nothing and nobody to the Heavyweight
    Champeenhood of the known world, alas, to be
Found "mysteriously" dead for seven nights and seven days

Oh Hail! Hail! Hail!
Jersey Joe Sugar Ray Floyd Patterson Kid Gavilan Archie Moore
Gentleman Jim John G. Chamber and the Marquis of Queensberry—
Oh, Hail to the Contest of Endurance!

IV.
Maybe I'm wrong and don't care if I am
But I believe I will
Sound the gong *Flam Flam Flam*
For the Great Brown Bomber who rose above the Buckalow Mountains
    and the hills of Alabam.

BORN: 1914 May 13th TAURUS:
First decanate: Sub-ruler, Venus
Constellation: LEPUS
Of Africa Indian and Caucasian blood
Making money making money making money FOR WHOM

The gong tolls?
MARVA! Fine brownskin middle-class fashion-struck woman prancing
    through celluloid cities of Paris, London, Madrid
Hanging out with Josephine Baker
    scream of a woman at ringside . . .

Jockstrap of the Bull!
Stalking Jabbing Stalking Jabbing Stalking Chunking bomb after bomb
    after bomb into the bodies of other men
    fighting as many as eight fights a year!
    1937 Chicago Knock out James J. Braddock
    1937 New York defeated Tommy Farr
    1938 New York Knock out Nathan Mann
    1938 New York Knock out Harry Thomas
    1938 New York Knock out Max Schmeling
    1939 New York Knock out John H. Lewis
    1939 Los Angeles Knock out Jack Roper
    1939 New York Knock out Tony Galento
    1939 Detroit Knock out Bob Paster
    1940 New York defeated Arturo Godey
    1940 New York Knock out Johnny Paycheck
    1940 New York Knock out Arturo Godey
    1940 Boston Joe Louis Knocked out Al McCoy
    1941 New York Joe Louis Knocked out Red Berman
    1941 Philadelphia Joe Louis Knocked out Gus Derazio

1941 Detroit Joe Louis Knocked out Abe Simon
1941 St. Louis Joe Louis Knocked out Tony Muste
1941 Washington D.C. Joe Louis whipped Buddy Baer
1941 New York Joe Louis Knocked out Billy Conn
1941 New York Joe Louis Knock out Lou Nova
1942 New York Joe Louis Knock out Buddy Baer
1942 New York Joe Louis Knock out Abe Simon
And then
    around the world
BROOM . . . BROOM . . . BRRRROOOOOOOOMMMMMMMMMMMM
                                PEARL HARBOR!
            UNCLE SAM WANTS YOU   boy
Uncle Sam God Damn Hush! yo mouf
          SLIP OF THE LIP MIGHT SINK A SHIP
          TODAY EUROPE TOMORROW THE WORLD
Exhibition fights for Uncle Sam's morale
But do not go near the white frenchy women, boy
Or you'll find your neck swinging from the ropes
scream of a woman . . .
          NOTHING TO FEAR BUT FEAR ITSELF
PATHE NEWS: Knockout Tojo: PATHE NEWS: All chickens cackle
when
    the ROOSTER crows: One down Two to go
PATHE NEWS: Atomic Bomb!
Hey, boy, you may be the Brown Bomber but we got a Bomb
that
        gonna
    knock out ten million chinks before you can throw a punch
Oh, Hail! Hail! Hail!
ATOMIC BOMB!

    V.
Stars and Stripes forever!
Five winters past
Stars and Stripes
Name a bottle of gin "Joe Louis"
    Spirit of Lightning
    The Knock Out Liquor

Five summertimes in the matador's ring
Taurus possessor of healing powers divinely given
Whom shall you fight five winter ages gone, Ole!

WEDNESDAY NIGHT JUNE 19TH 1945
YANKEE STADIUM
42,266 SPECTATORS FAN THE WITNESS BOX
1,925,564 DOLLARS RESIDE AT THE BOX OFFICE
Give us pause: Arthur Donovan all time fight referee
          Jo Humphreys all time fight announcer
    having died during the interim of the duration
Before the fight give them pause.

BILLY CONN FOOT FLEET NIMBLE FOR EIGHT ROUNDS
BACKING AWAY DANCING SIDE TO SIDE BACKPEDDLING BYCYCLING
NEW REFEREE EDDIE JOSEPH AS WELL AS THE NEW ANNOUNCER
ARE OUT OF BREATH TRYING TO KEEP APACE WITH THE SKATING
BUTTERFLY OF THE RING LADIES AND GENTLEMEN BUT NOW
EARLY IN THIS ROUND BILLY AINT MOVING FAST ENOUGH AND JOE
CATCHES HIM WITH A WICKED LEFT HOOK AND A SHARP
TEARING RIGHT HANDER

"He Can Run But He Can't Hide"

THE SECOND PUNCH, THE SHARP, TEARING RIGHT HANDER,
    RIPPED
OPEN A GASH UNDER THE BUTTERFLY'S LEFT EYE AND BILLY IS HURT
BUT NOT IN REAL TROUBLE NOT YET
NEVERTHELESS CONN'S LEGS DO NOT CARRY HIM BACKWARDS
    WITH THE
SAME EARLIER SPEED AND JOE IS ON TOP OF HIM ON TOP OF HIM
AND LOUIS HITS CONN FIVE FIVE FIVE FIVE FIVE PUNCHES IN
A BLISTERING FUSILLADE ALL IN THE SPACE OF SECONDS
AND ALL TO THE HEAD . . .

[Hey, Joe! Joe of Louis, why don't you come and go with me
Back down to Chattanooga Tennessee
I aint got a dime and I don't own a buffalo

But you and me Joe we are Tauruses We got hearts full of magnolias
      and lilacs and green grass in our loins
Face it everybody loves a winner but when you lose you lose alone
And it is cold out here among the pale stone
Please Joe
Come with me, do not let them drive you too like the rest
      into those anonymous ruins where
      haggard nurses stalk the silence
And forgotten men sit idle exhuming wisdom in
Oblivion's concern]

     . . . ALL TO THE HEAD
     THE LAST ONE IS A MURDEROUS RIGHT CROSS AND BILLY CONN SAGS
     LOUIS FIRES A HARD LEFT THAT STAGGERS CONN, AND FOLLOWS
     WITH A HARD LEFT AND RIGHT THAT STRETCHES CONN ON HIS
     BACK ON THE FLOOR WHERE REFEREE JOSEPH COUNTS HIM OUT
     FULL "TEN" AT TWO MINUTES NINETEEN SECONDS OF THE EIGHT
     AND FINAL ROUND
Final for Conn Final for Conn and Finally
An omen for you too Joe.

     VI.
So now we sit here in the year of nineteen hundred and seventy one.
What happened to all that money you made
What happened to your fortune
Oh, Birds! Birds! Birds!
We stand idle inside of trembling fists
      where no gongs
But the ringing in our spines limp and old

Yes, Old!

When first I journeyed from Chattanooga seeking strange
      insistent voices
To New York, expecting to actually find you walking the streets
      of Harlem, strong and proud and hear you speak to me alone
      characteristically as Billie Holiday might have spoken
      had she escaped,

I was disappointed.
Not with you but with the world!
For you are not merely my hero of old but hero of all time
     for all black men and women whirlwinding within the
     gift outraged;
But your friends, your wives, the multitude of hangers-on
Where are they—are they with you now?

I am with you Joe Louis
I am with you in your strange surroundings and in your fears,
     for, unbeknowning to those who write copy and those who put
     on parties,
Your fears are *my* fears—Oh, God! How real they really are!

Hail! Hail! Hail!
I walked with you when you were up and in
I walk with you now although you are out you are not down
     and never will
Oh, Hail! Great Brown Bomber born on the Buckalow Mountains
     among the Alabama Hills!

KO

WILLIAM HEYEN

Sometimes I have a general sense of where I'm going—a sound to keep following, or a shape on the page to keep filling out, or a story to work in and round toward, or a shifting combination of these. Sometimes I pretty much end up with what I decided I could or ought to do. But I'm most interested in poems that somehow find themselves somewhere they didn't know they'd be. They remind me of something that boxer Mike Tyson once said: "Everybody's got a plan until they're hit."

I've got a plan, but I'm hit. I'm staggering. I grope for the ropes, I'm hit again. The ropes don't support me, I fall. Maybe I get up and try to get the feeling in my legs back again. Maybe I stay down and out and at the end can't even hear the sound of the bell.

Relics

JOHN HILDEBIDLE

John L. Sullivan, in old age, in his arbor

The Boston Strong Boy chomps a dead stogey.
Hamfisted, barrelbellied monument,
in his grey and honored age he is serene
and tends leafy plants this bright autumn.
His broad open Irish face bears no mark,
not from Paddy Ryan, not from Corbett,
not from Bare-Knuckle Kilrain or the rest—
in his time he could take the hardest punch.
He always did his job of work, laying brick
or slugging for the title or even
play-acting Atlas in the vaudeville—
the great John L. gave you your nickel's worth,
a fine example to his noisy race.
So bighearted, honest, plainspoken, tough
but as his vines show, sensitive, he asked
no favors but took no cheap advantage,
kept his nose clean and bought his share of rounds,
and now, reformed, preaches for Temperance.
He scrapped his way into the history books
by beating proud men bloody with his fists.

From *The Iliad:* Boxing at the Funeral Games of Patroklas

HOMER

Translated from the Greek by Richmond Lattimore

'At boxing I won against Klytomedes, the son of Enops,
at wrestling against Angkaios of Pleuron, who stood up against me.
In the foot-race, for all his speed, I outran Iphiklos,
and with the spear I out-threw Polydoros and Phyleus.
It was only in the chariot-race that the sons of Aktor
defeated me, crossing me in the crowd, so intent on winning
were they, for the biggest prizes had been left for the horse-race.
Now these sons of Aktor were twins; one held the reins at his leisure,
held the reins at his leisure while the other lashed on the horses.
This was I, once. Now it is for the young men to encounter
in such actions, and for me to give way to the persuasion
of gloomy old age. But once I shone among the young heroes.
Go now, and honor the death of your companion with contests.
I accept this for you gratefully, and my heart is happy
that you have remembered me and my kindness, that I am not
        forgotten
for the honour that should be my honour among the Achaians.
May the gods, for what you have done for me, give you great happiness.'
He spoke, and Peleides went back among the great numbers
of Achaians assembled, when he had listened to all the praise spoken
by Neleus' son, and set forth the prizes for the painful boxing.
He led out into the field and tethered there a hard-working
six-year-old unbroken jenny, the kind that is hardest
to break; and for the loser set out a two-handled goblet.
He stood upright and spoke his word out among the Argives:
'Son of Atreus, and all you other strong-greaved-Achaians,
we invite two men, the best among you, to contend for these prizes
with their hands up for the blows of boxing. He whom Apollo
grants to outlast the other, and all the Achaians witness it,
let him lead away the hard-working jenny to his own shelter.
The beaten man shall take away the two-handled goblet.'

He spoke, and a man huge and powerful, well skilled in boxing,
rose up among them; the son of Panopeus, Epeios.
He laid his hand on the hard-working jenny, and spoke out:
'Let the man come up who will carry off the two-handled goblet.
I say no other of the Achaians will beat me at boxing
and lead off the jenny. I claim I am the champion. Is it not
enough that I fall short in battle? Since it could not be
ever, that a man could be a master in every endeavour.
For I tell you this straight out, and it will be a thing
     accomplished.
I will smash his skin apart and break his bones on each other.
Let those who care for him wait nearby in a huddle about him
to carry him out, after my fists have beaten him under.'
So he spoke, and all of them stayed stricken to silence.
Alone Euryalos stood up to face him, a godlike
man, son of lord Mckisteus of the seed of Talaos;
of him who came once to Thebes and the tomb of Oidipous after
his downfall, and there in boxing defeated all the Kadmeians.
The spear-famed son of Tydeus was his second, and talked to him
in encouragement, and much desired the victory for him.
First he pulled on the boxing belt about his waist, and then
gave him the thongs carefully cut from the hide of ranging
ox. The two men, girt up, strode into the midst of the circle
and faced each other, and put up their ponderous hands at the
     same time
and closed, so that their heavy arms were crossing each other,
and there was a fierce grinding of teeth, the sweat began to run
everywhere from their bodies. Great Epeios came in, and hit him
as he peered out from his guard, on the cheek, and he could no longer
keep his feet, but where he stood the glorious limbs gave.
As in the water roughened by the north wind a fish jumps
in the weeds of the beach-break, then the dark water closes above him,
so Euryalos left the ground from the blow, but great-hearted Epeios
took him in his arms and set him upright, and his true companions
stood about him, and led him out of the circle, feet dragging
as he spat up the thick blood and rolled his head over on one side.
He was dizzy when they brought him back and set him among them.
But they themselves went and carried off the two-handled goblet.

Joe Louis

LANGSTON HUGHES

Joe Louis is a man
For men to imitate—
When this country needed him,
He did not stall or fail.

Joe took up the challenge
And joined up for war.
Nobody had to ask him,
"What are you waiting for?"

As a private in the army
Of his talents he gave free
Two mighty boxing matches
To raise funds for liberty.

That's more than lots of others
Who still try to jim-crow Joe
Have either heart or mind to do—
So this is to let them know

That Joe Louis is a man for any man to imitate.
If everybody was like Joe Louis there'd be no
"Too little" or "too late."

To Be Somebody

LANGSTON HUGHES

Little girl
Dreaming of a baby grand piano
(Not knowing there's a Steinway bigger, bigger)
Dreaming of a baby grand to play
That stretches paddle-tailed across the floor,
Not standing upright
Like a bad boy in the corner,
But sending music
Up the stairs and down the stairs
And out the door
To confound even Hazel Scott
Who might be passing!

Oh!

Little boy
Dreaming of the boxing gloves
Joe Louis wore,
The gloves that sent
Two dozen men to the floor.
Knockout!
Bam! Bop! Mop!

There's always room,
They say,
At the top.

The Boxing Match

DAVID IGNATOW

Am I really a sports fan, I ask myself,
listening to the Dempsey-Firpo fight
over the radio and looking
at the open mouths of my friends:
Dempsey has just knocked Firpo out
of the ring, I am somewhat apathetic;
I can observe myself being surprised
but all the others are yelling with delight.
Of course I'm a sports fan, I assure myself.
Dempsey knocking Firpo out of the ring
is something I couldn't do. I could admit
that and admire strength. I fear it also
and I look around again and think
how if I scoffed at this hullabaloo
about a man being knocked out of the ring
these boys would turn on me and knock me down,
and I join in the yelling. Firpo
is climbing back into the ring
and I am glad for him
and admire him.

The Man Who Boxes

ANA ISTARÚ

Translated from the Spanish by Zoë Anglesey

He is being readied
so neatly: cheek-
bones of lead,
the quick ligaments
fine-tuned and violet nerves,
his irate arteries
(acrostic and circulatory
blood red and blue),
the splendid femurs reveal
his perfect disposition to love,
everything designed for this
is dancing with death.
A man canceling
his pact with the rose.
Crude, random-prone,
sober and frugal, death
wants his occipital bone,
the thistle of his tongue.
She undresses. She sucks
his vitreous drops,
leaving intact a filigree
of anisette sweat.
The man who boxes
brought his own slice of liver.
Death touches him,
loves him, wants
to rape him with her green
symmetric butterfly.
(Don't break apart,
sailor, not on your canvas deck.)
But death a death
probes between his temples.

The man who boxes
splits in two: there are two men
terrified, canceling
their pact with daybreak.
Spectators watch the man
see his x-ray.
Watching the man,
they don't see, don't see him.
Everyone came to stare at her,
to feel the spray of her saliva,
see her gangrene tongue
licking the nape of his neck,
her coal black tits.
At death, a death.
They pay for the velvety tickets.
Find their seats. Kiss each other.
They wait for the knockout.
The cornea's egg
splits like a live coal.
They pay to goad those
bullfighters, fools who bet
on uncorking cranial sockets,
his hothead, a skull
of calcium.
The man who boxes
apologizes, falls,
wants instant horns
to backup his knuckles.
But death gets up,
she won't step back
nor point her skeletal finger.
At ease in the spotlight
she intends something
irremediable, to french kiss
mouth to mouth.
And the man who boxes
apologizes, falls
already dead becoming one of the dead,

he leaves his home,
his body, memories,
for a finale of infinite farewells.
The man canceling
his pact with history.

Winner Joe (The Knock-Out King)

LIL JOHNSON

Joe Louis was born in Alabama
And raised up in Detroit
But he always had that feel and flow
Ever since he was a boy

So lay it Joe
You got the best go.

When Joe Louis fought in Chicago
Some bet that he would lose
But when the papers brought the news
He gave that kind of blue

So lay it Joe
You got the best go.

Levinsky made a few passes
And then he fell to the floor
Then the referee hollered "Hold it Joe"
For he won't be back no more.

So lay it Joe
You got the best go.

Ya'll heard about Primo Carnera
They thought he was so good
But Joe started choppin' on his head
Like a farmer choppin' wood.

So know it Joe
You got the best go.

Then Joe walked up to the man's mountain
And kindly shook his hand
Then Joe backed up a step or two
And knocked him in the promised land.

So knock it Joe
You got the best go.

Then Joe Louis went to New York
Just to fight that champion Baer
And before the fourth round ended up
Joe left him layin' there.

So lay it Joe
You got the best go.

But the Baer he took it easy
He didn't argue long
He went on back to California
And bought him a cattle farm.

He said, "Take it Joe"
You got the best go.

A Referee Toasts the Champion

Here's to the champion,
May he have bread when he's hungry,
Wine when he is dry,
Money when he wants it,
And heaven when he dies,
—Let her go!

The Boxers Embrace

RICHARD KATROVAS

In Prague or in New Orleans, my perfect night
of guilty pleasure is to watch a fight.

I know that it is heartless past all speech
to thrill at two men's pain as both must reach

across the bloody billion-year abyss
to strike the other one, or to make him miss.

Yet when I gaze upon the frank despair
of spirit-broken people who must bear

the torments of cool fiends they cannot see—
systemic meanness and brutality

of bureaucratic processes that hide
the facts of who has profited and lied—

I see inside the grotesque and plodding dance
of boxers something beautiful: a chance

to mediate the passions of the tribe
by what the ritual or fights describe

(as arm a sudden arc upon the gleam
within that space) for public fights redeem

our sense of being, at once, in and out
of nature, and so map the human route

across the razor's edge of slow extinction.
Such is the truth of all destructive action,

transcending histories of consequence
and serving therefore as a mottled lens

unto the bifurcated human heart
whose one true nature is to break apart

revealing beast and angel wrapping arms
beyond all consequence of temporal harms.

As systems fade, transform, reconstitute,
the fools will blather and the wise stand mute,

then innocence must suffer out of reach,
and over time our best intentions leach

through all the lies we hold as history.
No yearning human heart is ever free,

except when it has found its one true base:
where the last bell rings, and the boxers embrace.

Owed to Joe Louis

JOHN KIERAN

Babe Ruth could bat; Jess Owens, run; Red Grange could
    carry the ball;
At this and that and other things, Joe wouldn't be good at all.
But when he shuffles across the ring, there's this that I can
    tell:
His left to the chin is something like the kiss of a three-inch
    shell!

Now, Joe looks slow with the fast afoot or the wriggling
    human eel,
And it has been shown that his own chin is not casehardened
    steel;
But that and the rest we well may skip, for this one thing stands
    clear:
When he lands that left his victim drops like a stricken
    stockyard steer.

It's true that a punch could flatten Joe—and the peril still
    may run;
For strategy he may not be the best beneath the sun;
But for zing! and bing! (hark, the birdies sing!) there is this
    that I insist:
He can pack the power of dynamite in the brown-skinned human
    fist!

Joe isn't as smart as Einstein; there are things beyond his scope;
He never will sing like a Melchior or speak like a Bayard Swope.
But of all the men in all the world, J. Louis wins the crown
For throwing a leather thunderbolt and blasting a rival down!

(And what a poet I would be, and oh! the songs I'd sing,
If I could put the punch in rhyme that Joe puts in the ring!)

The House of Blue Light

DAVID KIRBY

Little Richard comes on the TV at Gold's Gym
    and the first thing that happens is, I burst into tears,
and the second thing is, I think to myself,
    I can't sing this music, but if I could,
I wouldn't accept a smidgen of public acclaim,

not one iota; rather, I'd be like
    19th-century French historian Fustel de Coulanges
entering a lecture hall to the applause of students
    and saying, "Do not applaud. It is not I who speak,
but history which speaks through me,"

and as I distract myself from my sorrow with this thought,
    pert "Today" show host Katie Couric
tries to cut Little Richard off,
    tries to get the camera on herself so she can go on
with the program, so she waves the crew back

and walks toward them to fill the lens and get away
    from Little Richard's hullabaloo, which is king-sized:
he's saying, "Turn me up! Turn me up!"
    and then, "All the beautiful women say, 'Woo woo!'"
and the women do say, "Woo woo!" and they are beautiful,

that crone there, this four-hundred-pounder,
    and then he says, "All the ol' ugly men say, 'Unnh!'"
and the men do say "Unnh!" and they are ugly,
    they're beasts, the stock brokers in their power ties,
even the slim, almost girlish delivery boys

are fat and hairy and proud to be that way,
    proud to be selfish and to take big craps,

and I'm crying and not sure whether I'm one
　　　　of the beautiful ones or the ugly,
and when I tell Barbara about this later,

she says, "It's an emotional time for you,
　　　　what with Ian going away to college,"
and I see what she means,
　　　　　　　because at least part of my Gold's Gym sorrow
is due to the fact that tomorrow I'll say good-bye

to this boy I've had a steak-and-egg breakfast with
　　　　practically every Saturday morning of his life,
and now he's going away, which he should,
　　　　　　　though why Little Richard would trigger my tears,
I have no idea, except, come to think of it,

for the strong, indeed necessary, tie between
　　　　pop music and sentiment, as evidenced by the last time
I boohooed like a li'l weiner while listening to pop songs,
　　　　which was after Roy Orbison had died
and, as part of a tribute show, the DJ had played,

not only Roy Orbison singing "Danny Boy,"
　　　　an Irish father's farewell to his only son
when he goes off to fight in the foreign wars,
　　　　　　　but also the seldom-heard reply, which is the song
Danny Boy sings at his father's graveside when he comes back

and finds that, irony of ironies,
　　　　while he has survived sabre blow and cannon fire,
Old Age, the surest of Death's warriors,
　　　　　　　has crept up on his dad and cut him down
as lethally as any of the English King's artillerymen,

and now I see Ian in his farmboy's worsteds,
　　　　leaning on his musket and salting the stones
of my grave with his bitter tears. . . .

My son, me, Little Richard, Roy Orbison:
it's a mishmash, for sure—

certainly it's a step into the House of Blue Light,
        the place where Miss Molly rocks
and that is not a house of prostitution,
        which would involve a light
of a different color altogether, but a fun house,

a good-time house, yet a house where
        the unexpected occurs, sort of like that place
Muhammad Ali called "the near room,"
        whose door would open in the middle of a round,
and part of Ali would be whaling the tar

out of an opponent and part would be looking
        into that room, where he'd see orange alligators
playing saxophones and dancing snakes
        with green hats on their heads,
and he'd want to go in there, want to party

with these bebop reptiles and groove-ball amphibians,
        when suddenly whup whup whup whup! his opponent
would remind him what he was there for,
        and Ali would have to whupwhupwhupwhupwhupwhup!
and take care of business real fast

and shower and have a news conference
        and then go home and wonder what he saw
in that room there with all that crazy stuff in it,
        including some things he's seen before
and some he's never seen and some he hopes to see again

and some he can't bear to think about
        even though he's home now, got his feet up
on the Danish Modern coffee table and a nice cold glass
        of fruit juice in his hand.
He's been somewhere, that's for sure!

He's been on an "expedition,"
        a word I recently heard pronounced
as "eks-pay-DEE-shone" by an Italian biologist
        who was telling me about his latest trip to Antarctica
and who is probably the last person to have said

this word to my face since my brother Albert
        forty-five years ago when I was seven and he ten
and we used to play this game called African Ranger
        in the woods that surrounded our parents' house,
the one we had to sell when my parents got too old

to keep it up, the two sons talking on the porch
        as the mother sweeps and tidies and the father,
who has not cried at anything since the death
        of his own parents decades earlier, sobs in the study
as he says good-bye to his books, and it is late afternoon

in the early days of winter, and there is no part of the world
        gloomier than the bayou country at that time of the year,
and Albert says to me, "Want to play African Ranger?"
        and it takes me a minute to remember the game,
which consisted of starting out on an "expedition"

but soon turned into two shirtless boys shooting blunt arrows
        into each other's hides, and I say, "Nope,"
and he says, "Me, either," and the last piece of light
        falls out of the sky, and it's dark out there,
the woods are black; you could walk into them, if you wanted,

and a little path would take you farther and farther
        from your old life, and soon you'd see this cottage,
and there'd be music coming out of it, and you'd look in,
        and Little Richard would be there and Ali
and Roy Orbison and yourself when you were a child

but also a teenager and a young man, too,
    and everybody'd be talking and laughing,
and somebody would look up and see you as you are now,
    and they'd all wave and say,
Hey there, we've been waiting for you, come on in.

Boxing Day

YUSEF KOMUNYAKAA

Burns never landed a blow.
It was hopeless, preposterous, heroic.
—Jack London

This is where Jack Johnson
cornered Tommy Burns in 1908.
Strong as an ironbark
tree, he stood there
flexing his biceps
till he freed
the prisoner under his skin.
    The bell clanged
    & a profusion of voices
    shook the afternoon. Johnson
jabbed with the power
of an engine throwing a rod,
& Burns sleepwalked
to the spinning edge
of the planet like a moth
drawn to a burning candle.
He was dizzy as a drunken girl
tangoing with a flame tree
breaking into full bloom,
burdened by fruits of desire
& the smell of carnival.
    A currawong crossed the sun
    singing an old woman's cry.
    The referee threw in his towel
    in the fourteenth round & bookies
    scribbled numbers beside names
    madly, as twenty thousand rose
    into the air like a wave.
For years the razor-gang boys
bragged about how they would've KOed

Johnson, dancing & punching each day.
Eighty years later, the stadium's
checkered with tennis courts,
a plantation of pale suits
called White City.
  I hear Miles Davis' trumpet
  & Leadbelly's "Titanic."
  A bell's metal treble
  reverberates . . . the sunset
  moves like a tremble of muscle
  across Rushcutters Bay,
  back to the name Johnson
flashing over the teletype
when he danced The Eagle Rock,
drove fast cars & had a woman
on each arm, to Jesse Willard
pushing him down into a whirlpool's
death roll under white
confetti & cheers in Havana.

Titanic

LEADBELLY

It was midnight on the sea
Band playing "nearer my God to thee—"
Cryin', fare thee, Titanic, fare thee well.

Titanic, when it got its load,
Captain hollered, "All Aboard"
Cryin', fare thee, Titanic, fare thee well.

Jack Johnson want to get on board,
Captain said, "I ain't haulin' no coal"
Cryin', fare thee, Titanic, fare thee well.

Titanic was comin' 'round the curve
When it ran into that great big iceberg
Cryin', fare thee, Titanic, fare thee well.

Titanic was sinking down,
Had them lifeboats all around.
Cryin', fare thee, Titanic, fare thee well.

Had them lifeboats around,
Savin' the women and children, lettin' the men go down.
Cryin', fare thee, Titanic, fare thee well.

Jack Johnson heard the mighty shock,
Might 'a' seen him doin' the Eagle Rock.
Cryin', fare thee, Titanic, fare thee well.

When the women and children got on the land,
Cryin', "Lord have mercy on my man."
Fare thee, Titanic, fare thee well.

After His Athletic Father's Death

CHARLES LEVENDOSKY

and at forty
he begins to jog at dawn,
in the nearing light,
a dark figure in navy sweatsuit
pacing himself around the park.

his breath hangs before him
in the cold air
                    a foggy presence
he chases, runs through,
inhales and exhales.

those tropic afternoons
boxing with his father,
lifting weights,
and running out for a pass;
a little fat boy hating to move.

at forty begins to jog,
breathing hard, ache in the calves,
bounce of brain against skull,
and footfalls in his ears.
his hands form jogger's fists

that jab through his ghostly breath;
a heavyweight in training
as his father had been, once.
hears footfalls, barely turns to glimpse
the hanging mist over his shoulder.

Baby Villon

PHILIP LEVINE

He tells me in Bangkok he's robbed
Because he's white; in London because he's black;
In Barcelona, Jew; in Paris, Arab;
Everywhere and at all times, and he fights back.

He holds up seven thick little fingers
To show me he's rated seventh in the world,
And there's no passion in his voice, no anger
In the flat brown eyes flecked with blood.

He asks me to tell all I can remember
Of my father, his uncle; he talks of the war
In North Africa and what came after,
The loss of his father, the loss of his brother,

The windows of the bakery smashed and the fresh bread
Dusted with glass, the warm smell of rye
So strong he ate till his mouth filled with blood.
"Here they live, here they live and not die,"

And he points down at his black head ridged
With black kinks of hair. He touches my hair,
Tells me I should never disparage
The stiff bristles that guard the head of the fighter.

Sadly his fingers wander over my face,
And he says how fair I am, how smooth.
We stand to end this first and last visit.
Stiff, 116 pounds, five feet two,

No bigger than a girl, he holds my shoulders,
Kisses my lips, his eyes still open,
My imaginary brother, my cousin,
Myself made otherwise by all his pain.

The Right Cross

PHILIP LEVINE

The sun rising over the mountains
found me awake, found an entire valley
of sleepers awake, dreaming of a few hours
more of sleep. Though the Great Central Valley
is home for the homeless, the fruit pickers
of creation, for runaway housewives
bored by their husbands, and bored husbands,
the rising sun does not dip back behind
the Sierras until we're ready. The Valley sun
just comes on. We rise, drop our faces
in cold water, and face the prospects
of a day like the last one from which we
have not recovered. All this month I've
gone in search of the right cross, the punch
which had I mastered it forty years ago
might have saved me from the worst. The heavy bag
still hangs from the rafters of the garage,
turning in no wind, where my youngest son
left it when he went off ten years ago
abandoning his childish pursuits to me.
After tea, dry toast, and some toe-touching,
I'm ready to work. I pull on the salty
bag gloves, bow my head, dip one shoulder

into the great sullen weight, and begin
with a series of quick jabs. I'm up
on my toes, moving clockwise, grunting
as the blows crumple, the air going out
and coming back in little hot benedictions.
I'm remembering Nate Coleman barking
all those years ago, "Straight from the shoulder,
Levine," as though describing his own nature.
The gentlest man I ever knew, perfect
with his fists, our master and mentor,

who fought only for the love of it,
living secretly by day in suit and tie,
vending copper cookware from the back seat
of his black Plymouth. The dust rises
from the sour bag, and I feel how fragile
my left wrist has become, how meek the bones
of my shoulders as the shocks come home,
the bag barely moving. "Let it go!"
Nate would call, urging the right hand out
against the big light heavies, Marvin
with his sudden feints and blunt Becker,
his face grim and closed behind cocked fists.
Later, the gym gone silent in the half-dark,
Nate would stand beside me, left hand
on my shoulder, and take my right wrist
loosely in his right hand, and push it out
toward an imagined foe, his right knee
pressed behind my right knee until my leg
came forward. I could feel his words
—"like this"—falling softly on my cheek
and smell the milky sweetness of his breath
—"you just let it go"—, the dark lashes
of his mysterious green eyes unmoving.
The bag is going now, swinging easily
with the force of jabs and hooks. The garage
moans as though this dance at its center
threatened to bring it down. I throw a right,
another, and another before I take my rest
in the cleared space amid the detritus
of five lives: boxes of unanswered letters,
school papers, report cards, scattered parts
of lawn mowers and motorcycles gone to ground.
The sky is coming through the mismatched boards
of the roof, pure blue and distant, the day
rising from the oily cement of the floor
as again I circle the heavy bag throwing out
more punches until I can't. If my sons
were here they'd cheer me on, and I'd

keep going into the impossible heat
and before I quit I might throw, just once,
for the first time, the perfect right cross.
They say it's magic. When it lands
you feel the force of your whole body,
even the deeper organs, the dark fluids
that go untapped for decades, the tiny
pale microbes haunting the bone marrow,
the intricate patterns that devised
the bones of the feet, you feel them
finally coming together like so many
atoms of salt and water as they form
an ocean or a tear, for just an instant
before the hand comes back under the chin
in its ordinary defensive posture.
The boys, the grown men dreaming
of the squared circle into which the light
falls evenly as they move without effort
hour after hour, breathing easily, oiled
with their own sweat, fight for nothing
except the beauty of their own balance,
the precision of each punch.
I hated to fight. I saw each blow
in a sequence of events leading
finally to a winner and a loser.
Yet I fought as boys were told to do,
and won and lost as men must. That's over.
Six months from my sixtieth year, doused
in my own juices, I call it quits
for the day, having earned the rituals—
the long bath, the shave, the laundered clothes,
the afternoon muse as the little clots
of stiffness break up and travel down
the channels of the blood. After dinner
and before sleep, I walk behind the garage
among grape vines and swelling tomatoes
to where the morning glories close down
in the rising darkness and the cosmos

flare their brilliant whites a last time
before the moon comes out. From under
the orange trees the click and chuckle
of quail; the tiny chicks dart out
for a last look and scurry back again
before the earth goes gray. A dove moans,
another answers from a distant yard as though
they called each other home, called each of us
back to our beds for the day's last work.

Shadow Boxing

PHILIP LEVINE

That man with the cat face circling the ring,
long spidery arms at his sides, is Gavilan,
oiled and ready, the one-time cane cutter
now fine-tuned to destroy. He's waiting.
If someone would step up, he'd hold down
the rope's middle strand, extend a hand,
then stare down with unblinking, bloodshot,
almond eyes. The dusty light of August
1948 falls across the Kid's bronzed shoulders
as now he dances counter-clockwise flicking
out first a left, then a right. "Estamos listo,"
says the bald trainer.
                  "Ready or not,"
is what I heard. I stayed less than a month
in Havana, slept late, ate only Chinese
to make my money last, drank rum straight,
walked evenings by the great harbor
where the sea spread out, blackening
around the first shivering stars. The delicate
pale roses and ochers of the castle walls
and the echoing cathedral vanished into
shadows by the time I gave up and turned
through the mid-night streets to find
the Calle Real, the Hotel Obisbo, the past.

To a Fighter Killed in the Ring

LOU LIPSITZ

In a gym in Spanish Harlem
boys with the eyes of starved leopards
flick jabs at your ghost
chained to a sandbag.

They smell in the air the brief truth of poverty
just as you once did:
                              "The weak don't get rich."

You made good.
Probably you were a bastard,
dreaming of running men down in a Cadillac
and tearing blouses off women.

And maybe in your dreams great black teeth
ran after you down dead-end alleyways
and the walls of your room
seemed about to collapse,
bringing with them a sky of garbage
and your father's leather strap.
And you sat up afraid you were dying
just as you had so many nights as a child.

Small bruises to the brain.
An accumulation
of years of being hit.

I will not forget that picture of you
hanging over the ropes, eyes closed,

completely wiped out.
Like a voice
lost in the racket of a subway train
roaring on under the tenements of Harlem.

Epigrams

LUCILIUS

Translated from the Latin by Humbert Wolfe

I.

This Olympicus who is now such as you see him, Augustus, once had a nose, a chin, a forehead, ears and eyelids. Then becoming a professional boxer he lost all, not even getting his share of his father's inheritance; for his brother presented a likeness of him he had and he was pronounced to be a stranger, as he bore no resemblance to it.

II.

Having such a mug, Olympicus, go not to a fountain nor look into any transparent water, for you, like Narcissus, seeing your face clearly, will die, hating yourself to death.

III.

When Ulysses after twenty years came safe to his home, Argos the dog recognized his appearance when he saw him, but you, Stratophon, after boxing for four hours, have become not only unrecognizable to dogs but to the city. If you will trouble to look at your face in the glass, you will say on your oath, "I am not Stratophon."

IV.

Your head, Apollophanes, has become a sieve, or the lower edge of a worm-eaten book, all exactly like ant-holes, crooked and straight, or musical notes Lydian and Phrygian. But go on boxing without fear; for even if you are struck on the head you will have the marks you have— you can't have more.

V.

Cleombrotus ceased to be a pugilist, but afterwards married, and now has at home all the blows of the Isthmian and Nemean games, a pugnacious old woman hitting as hard as in the Olympian fights, and he dreads his own house more than ever he dreaded the ring. Whenever he gets his wind, he is beaten with all the strokes known in every match to make him pay her his debt; and if he pays it, he is beaten again.

VI.

His competitors set up here the statue of Apis the boxer, for he never hurt anyone.

VII.

I, Androleos, took part in every boxing contest that the Greeks preside over, every single one. At Pisa I saved one ear, and in Plataea one eyelid, but at Delphi I was carried out insensible. Damoteles, my father, and my fellow-townsmen had been summoned by herald to bear me out of the stadium either dead or mutilated.

VIII.

Onesimus the boxer came to the prophet Olympus wishing to learn if he were going to live to old age. And he said, "Yes, if you give up the ring now, but if you go on boxing, Saturn is your horoscope."

The Time Is Two, Not Three

NORMAN MAILER

Punch up
   and counter
      by two's
         said the
         boxer
         who was dead
            half-dead
         for he knew
         the combo
            was three
Like we
   he deigned
   to waltz
He spewed up
   his salts
   like we.
God
   give us life
      by three
He won't.
He's dead
   from knuckle
      to knee
We killed Him
Thee and me
   tender lovers
   missing three
Too late
   a daughter
Never a son
The moon
   is begotten
but the lies

not done
we were less
than God
So he dared
us all
Now the world
will die
for lack
of a ball.

From *The Setup*

JOSEPH MONCURE MARCH

A fighter's life is short at best.
No time to waste;
No time to rest.
The spotlight shifts:
The clock ticks fast:
All youth become old age at last.
All fighters weaken.
All fighters crack.
All fighters go—
And they never come back.
Well—
So it goes:
Time hits the hardest blows.

Joe Louis Blues

CARL MARTIN

Now listen all you prize fighters : who don't want to
    meet defeat
Take a tip from me : stay off Joe Louis' beat
Now he won all his fights : twenty-three or four
And left twenty of his opponents : lying on the floor
They all tried to win : but the test was too hard
When he laid the hambone : couple jumped out for it
Listen all you prize fighters : don't play him too cheap
If he lands with either hand : he'll sure put you to the seat
Now he packs dynamite in his left : he carries a punching
    right
He's the one will make you balky : or as high as a kite
He charges on his opponents : from the beginning of the gong
He batters them into submission : then they all sing a song
I bet on the Brown Bomber : for he knows his stuff
And lays it on his opponents : until he get enough
Now he's a natural born fighter : who likes to fight them all
The bigger they come : he says the harder they fall
That terrific left : boys is all he needs
But that six-inch right : come with lightning speed
Listen all you prize fighters : don't play him too cheap
Take a tip from me : stay off Joe Louis' beat

From *The Everlasting Mercy:* Wood Top Fields

JOHN MASEFIELD

And springy to a Boxer's feet;
At Harvest hum the moon so bright
Did shine on Wood Top for the fight . . .
The stakes were drove, the ropes were hitched,
Into the ring my hat I pitched . . .
                                    . . . Time!

From the beginning of the bout
My luck was gone, my hand was out.
Right from the start Bill called the play,
But I was quick and kept away
Till the fourth round, when work was mixed,
And then I knew Bill had me fixed.
My hand was out, why, Heaven knows;
Bill punched me when and where he chose.
Through two more rounds we quartered wide
And all the time my hands were tied;
Bill punched me when and where he pleased,
The cheering from my backers ceased,
But every punch I heard a yell
Of 'That's the style, Bill, give him hell.'
No one for me, but Jimmy's light
'Straight left! Straight left!' and 'Watch his right.'

I don't know how a boxer goes
When all his body hums from blows;
I know I seemed to rock and spin,
I don't know how I saved my chin . . .
But in the ninth, with pain and knocks
I stopped: I couldn't fight nor box.
Bill mixed his swing, the light was tricky.
But I went down, and stayed down, dicky.
'Get up,' cried Jim. I said 'I will.'
Then all the gang yelled, 'Out him, Bill.

Out him.' Bill rushed . . . and Clink, Clink, Clink.
Time! And Jim's knee, and rum to drink.
And round the ring there ran a titter:
'Saved by the call, the bloody quitter.'

They drove (a dodge that never fails)
A pin beneath my finger nails.
They poured what seemed a running beck
Of cold spring water down my neck;
Jim with a lancet quick as flies
Lowered the swellings round my eyes.
They sluiced my legs and fanned my face
Through all that blessed minute's grace;
Then gave my calves a thorough kneading,
They salved my cuts and stopped the bleeding.
A gulp of liquor dulled the pain,
And then the two flasks clinked again.
Time!
      There was Bill as grim as death.
He rushed, I clinched, to get more breath.
And breath I got, though Billy bats
Some stinging short-arms in my slats.
And when we broke, as I foresaw,
He swung his right in for the jaw.
I stopped it on my shoulder bone,
And at the shock I heard Bill groan—
A little groan or moan or grunt—
As though I'd hit his wind a bunt.
At that I clinched, and while we clinched,
His old-time right-arm dig was flinched,
And when we broke he hit me light
As though he couldn't trust his right,
He flapped me somehow with his wrist
As though he couldn't use his fist,
And when he hit he winced with pain.
I thought, 'Your sprained thumb's crocked again.'
So I got strength and Bill gave ground,
And that round was an easy round.
During the wait my Jimmy said,

'What makes Billy fight so dead?
He's all to pieces. Is he blown?'
'His thumb's out.'
                    'No? Then it's your own.
It's all your own, but don't be rash—
He's got the goods if you've got cash,
And what one hand can do he'll do,
Be careful this next round or two.'

Time! There was Bill, and I felt sick
That luck should play so mean a trick
And give me leave to knock him out
After he'd plainly won the bout . . .
Bill took that pain without a sound
Till half way through the eighteenth round,
And then I sent him down and out,
And Silas said, 'Kane wins the bout.'
When Bill came to, you understand,
I ripped the mitten from my hand
And went across to ask Bill shake,
My limbs were all one pain and ache . . .
Bill in his corner bathed his thumb,
Buttoned his shirt, and glowered glum.
'I'll never shake your hand', he said.
'I'd rather see my children dead.
I've been about and had some fun with you,
But you're a liar and I've done with you . . .
That put my meaning clear, I guess,
Now get to hell; I want to dress.'

I dressed. My backers one and all
Said, 'Well done you,' or 'Good old Saul.'
'Saul is a wonder and a fly 'un,
What'll you have, Saul, at the "Lion"?'
With merry oaths they helped me down
The stony wood-path to the town.

Fist Fighter

DAN MASTERSON

(based on George Bellows' painting: "Stag at Sharkey's")
*("Saloon-keeper Tom Sharkey, retired heavyweight contender, is doing some
fancy footwork in avoiding the current NYC ban on boxing by awarding
'membership' to every fighter he books for his Athletic Club brawls in his Lincoln
Square cellar."*—The New York Times, *1909)*

The kid comes down Sharkey's stairs slapping
Snow off his great-coat, the threadbare elbows
Sporting ragtag patches cut from the hem.
He's got a fresh shiner from one of the 3 other
Smokers he's already worked tonight & a few
Random welts starting to fade. He weaves his way

Through the crowd, nods to Sharkey, unlocks
The Stay Out door, & flicks the wall switch
Before closing the door behind him. He hangs
His coat on a hook near the speed bag, & turns
It into a blur with a flurry of lefts & rights. He
Steps out of his trousers, reties his trunks & slips

A fold of 1's into an envelope: 15 of them,
5 bucks a win. He sticks it under the mattress
He falls down on & closes his eyes for no more
Than a 10-count. Up on his feet, peeling off
His tee shirt sopped in sweat & spattered with
Someone else's blood, he rubs his arms & yanks

A clean tee shirt on as he leaves the only room
Sharkey rents: half the kid's take per week.
A dime for each piece of skinny-wood he burns
In the potbelly. 2 dimes for a hot bath upstairs.

Free beer if Sharkey goes out on the town. Sneaked
Meals from the cook, Bernie, who calls the kid

Champ and takes his break at 10 o'clock, in time
To see the kid do his stuff. The main room's filthy:
6 rows of metal chairs tight against a 9′ × 9′ ring
Strung with braided clothesline covered in black
Tape. 10 100-watt clear bulbs hang limp on their
Bare wires, sawdust wet on the concrete floor,

The potbelly's stovepipe jammed through the broken
Glass of an overhead window nailed shut & painted
Brown, an open drain in a far corner: Sharkey's "Please
Flush" sign a ten-year-old bad joke, stale beer sticky
Underfoot, cigar smoke & old men with nowhere
To go. The kid's heading for the ring, lifting 2 rolls

Of waxed-gauze from their pegs & 2 hollow stubs
Of hose to support his closed fists. He wraps his hands
As though they are already bleeding, round and round,
Flexing his fingers as the knuckles grow padded and tight:
The only gloves Sharkey allows. Just 18, the kid's in his
4th season, & his pale Irish grin, riding above thick shoulders,

Is clean except for some hack doctor's stitch marks
Under the left cheekbone. He climbs through the ropes &
Sits on the stool, fondling his mouthpiece, & studies
The empty stool across the ring, wondering who it will be,
& now there's Harris stepping through the ropes, his
Bare knuckles showing through the gauze: a leftover

Wrap-job from his earlier fight down the block
Somewhere. Getting too old for this stuff, 37, 38,
Starting to lose his edge. It'll be okay, thinks
The kid. He decked Harris in minute 6 last night
At Ramsey's & he's got no defense left, just a pecking
Jab & a giveaway right that opens him up for rib shots

That put him down & a jelly belly to keep him down.
Sharkey's playing ref again, calling them to the center
Of the ring: No gouging, kneeing, biting, wrestling, butting,
Hitting low, no clock. You want out, you stay down for 10.
Go.

He's in the Ring

MEMPHIS MINNIE MCCOY

Hey all you peoples going out tonight : just going to
  see Joe Louis fight
And if you ain't got no money : have to go tomorrow night
Crying he even carried a mean left : and he carried a mean right
And if he hits you with either one : same as a charge from a
  dynamite
I'm going to tell all of you prize fighters : don't play Joe for no fool
If he hits you with that left duke : same as a kick from a Texas
  mule
Joe Louis is a two-fist fighter : and he stands six feet tall
And the bigger they come : he say the harder they fall
Boys if I only had ten hundred dollars : I'd a-laid it up on my shelf
I'd bet anybody pass my house : that one round Joe would knock
  him out
I wouldn't even pay my house rent : I wouldn't buy me nothing
  to eat
Joe Louis would take a chance with them : I would put you on
  your feet

The Nonpareil's Grave

M. J. MCMAHON

Far out in the wilds of Oregon,
    On a lonely mountain side,
Where Columbia's mighty waters
    Roll down to the ocean side;
Where the giant fir and cedar
    Are imaged in the wave,
O'er grown with firs and lichens,
    I found Jack Dempsey's grave.

I found no marble monolith,
    No broken shaft, or stone,
Recording sixty victories,
    This vanquished victor won;
No rose, no shamrock could I find
    No mortal here to tell
Where sleeps in this forsaken spot
    Immortal Nonpareil.

A winding wooden canyon road
    That mortals seldom tread,
Leads up this lonely mountain
    To the desert of the dead.
And the Western sun was sinking
    In Pacific's golden wave,
And those solemn pines kept watching,
    Over poor Jack Dempsey's grave.

Forgotten by ten thousand throats,
    That thundered his acclaim,
Forgotten by his friends and foes,
    Who cheered his very name.
Oblivion wraps his faded form,
    But ages hence shall save

The memory of that Irish lad
    That fills poor Dempsey's grave.

Oh, Fame, why sleeps thy favored son
    In wilds, in woods, in weeds,
And shall he ever thus sleep on,
    Interred his valiant deeds?
'Tis strange New York should thus forget
    Its "bravest of the brave"
And in the fields of Oregon,
    Unmarked, leave Dempsey's grave.

Sonny Liston

JAY MEEK

Floored in the bedroom of his home
in Vegas, on the table his revolver
in its holster, ready for an enemy,
he'd run out of chances: his hook
lost its shock, arms turned to flab,
his purse got tighter. When he blew
Clay's fight in that Maine mill-town,
too suddenly downed, bartenders said:
"Next time he's gonna fight some fruit
from a garbage scow on the Atlantic.
Out there he can really take a dive."
At the end, slow-footed and wooden,
he banged through stables of punks
and with each bout his ratings dove.
He was eighth. Below, a Venezuelan,
and a Basque named Urtain who lifted
stones. At ten they stop counting.

The Seventh Round

JAMES MERRILL

Give it to him!
To you, you mean.
As always (mezzanine
Gone dazzling dim,

A crown at stake)
Before you stands
The giver with clenched hands.
Drop your own. Take.

Sonny Liston

E. ETHELBERT MILLER

they cut the gloves off and i'm free
my face swollen no less than my reputation
two hands held my life together
i was nothing until i had to fight to live
now a young kid comes out of nowhere
calls me ugly and a bear
my stare once cut men before they entered the ring
i could smell fear dripping on the lacing of their shoes
i was a fighter and champion when colored people
were satisfied with much less
i've seen a lot of men sit on stools and never move
i learned to take a punch and how to knock a man out
in two rounds
i don't need to talk much
the world ain't pretty and a lot of people try to hide
too bad the night has a thousand eyes

Irises at Ringside

JOHN MINCZESKI

They start life as boxing gloves
and end with the smell of bridesmaids.
Will they ever wear these things again?

Undefeated Heavyweight, 20 Years Old

JOYCE CAROL OATES

I.

Never been hurt! never
knocked down! or staggered or
stunned or made to know there's a blow
to kill not his own!—therefore the soul
glittering like jewels worn
on the outside of the body.

II.

A boy with a death's-head mask dealing hurt
in an arc of six short inches. Unlike ours
his flesh recalls its godhead, if dimly. Unlike
us he knows he will live forever.

The walloping sounds of his body blows are iron
striking bone.
The joy he promises is of a fist breaking bone.
For whose soul is so bright, so burnished,
so naked in display?

All insult, says this death's-head—ancient, tribal,
last week's on the street—is redeemed in the taste
of another's blood.

You don't know. But you know.

"Angel Firpo" Waltz

SALOMON PACORAH

Al pugilista Argentine Luis Angel Firpo

sing   their prize ring king   all   day.
far   a liv — ing star   is   he.

Chorus
An — gel Fir — po waltz _____ Eve — ry

cresc.
one sing in praise of his glo — ry ___ one and all

knows   him   And   for   him

Boxers Hit Harder When Women Are Around

KENNETH PATCHEN

The sleeping face folds down over this human country
And a battle crackles through the fat, blue air above us.

Rock-a-bye poor ladies, the world was ever cruel and wrong . . .
And while you sleep, be sure your sons will make a mess of
    something.

Ho! ho! my hovering leopard. Ho! my hungry dogs . . .
Inspect my savage house;
Here the moth-bladed light stabs at fake, lancing remote lies.

Do they stir in their troubled sleep?
Somebody will always look out for my poor ladies . . .
Rock-a-bye my darlings, the world won't always be wrong,

The sleeping face folds down over the broken harlot
Who stands behind the plough unshakeable,
Bewildered as all the bells in the world thunder
Against the castles where chained tigers await
The tread of the Huntsman from whose hand they will feed,
From whose desperate heart will flower a manflame honor.

Who fights the gunclan will wear hard gloves and come out
    fighting . . .
And it won't seem so lonesome when the lights are all on.

1 Corinthians 9:25–27

ST. PAUL

Everyone who competes in the games goes into strict training. They train to get a wreath that will not last; but we train to get a wreath that will last forever.

Therefore I do not run like a man running aimlessly; I do not fight like a man shadowboxing.

No, I beat my body and make it my slave so that after I have preached to others, I myself will not be disqualified for the prize.

To Let Go

MICHAEL PETTIT

I am tired of training.
—Muhammad Ali

At the Agricultural Experiment Station
the boys are all over me the morning after:
no one missed the licking you took.
Their fists are up; they bob, weave, dance
forward and back. Each face is happy
under its hat. I pay off my bets,

thinking of Gary Scheiss, who waited tables
on his knees the last time you got beat.
I want to eat all the apple cobbler
and drink all the sweet cream. Who
has not dreamed to let go? So I grin
back as the boys count you out again.
You, still asleep this morning, the tip
Of your tongue wetting your bruised lips.

Olympia 7

PINDAR

Translated from the Greek by Richmond Lattimore

As one who takes a cup from a lavish hand,
bubbling within the foam of the grape,
presenting it
to a young bridegroom, pledging hearth to hearth, the pride,
   sheer gold, of possession,
the joy of the feat, to honor his new son, render him
among friends present admired for the bride's consent:

so I, bringing poured nectar of victory,
gift of the Muses, the mind's sweet yield,
offer it up
to the conquerors at Olympia and Pytho. Blessed is he whom
   good fame surrounds.
Grace eyes one man, then another, bestowing favor
Frequently to the melodious lyre and the manifold music of
   flutes;

and to both strains I keep company with Diagoras, singing
the sea's child, daughter of Aphrodite and bride of Helios,
   Rhodes,
and give praise, spoil of his boxing, to the onslaught of a
   man gigantic,
wreathed in victory beside Alpheos' water
and Kastalia; and to Damagetos his father, darling of
   Justice,
who dwell in the triple-cited island over against
the jut of broad Asia, by right of an Argive spear.

I will try to straighten the story from the beginning
with news from as far back as Tlepolemos
for Herakles'

race of reaching strength. On the father's side they glory
   in Zeus' descent; on the mother's,
Amyntoridai from Astydameia. Delusions innumerable
hang their shadows over men's minds. This thing passes wit
   to discover,

what is best now and at the end for a man to attain.
Even Tlepolemos, this island's founder, once
angered, rearing
the stock of brute olive, smote to death Alkmana's bastard
   brother,
Likymnios, at Tiryns as he issued from the chamber of Midea.
   Despair in the brain has driven
even the wise man out of his course. He went to the god for
   counsel.

From the fragrant sanctuary the gold-haired god bespoke a
   voyage
of ships from the Lernaian ness straight for a seagirt reach,
where once the high king of the gods drenched their city in
   a gold snowfall,
when, by the artifice of Hephaistos,
at the stroke of the bronze-heeled axe Athene sprang
from the height of her father's head with a strong cry.
The sky shivered before her and earth our mother.

Then Hyperion's giant son, light-giver to mortals,
laid a necessity upon his own children
to guard thereafter:
they must be first to found a bright altar to the goddess and
   establish a stately sacrifice
and propitiate the heart of her father and the maid of the
   ringing spear. Respect
for forethought puts on men godliness and delight also.

Yet the unpredictable mist of forgetfulness stalks us,
it wrenches aside the right way of action
far from our thoughts.

Thus they went up, having not the bright seed of flame, with
   fireless sacrament they appointed
the grove on the acropolis. Yet he, assembling the yellow cloud,
rained much gold upon them, and the green-eyed goddess granted

every art, that they should surpass all men in the excellent
   work of their hands.
And their streets grew images in the likeness of men and beasts.
Their fame went deep. For the wise skill will wax greater for
   its innocence.
The ancient legends of men
tell how, when Zeus and the immortals divided the earth
Rhodes had not yet shone in the sea's water,
but the island was hidden in the salt depths.

Helios was gone, and none showed forth his lot.
They left him with no guerdon of land,
that blameless god.
He spoke, and Zeus would cast again, but Helios would not suffer
   it, for he said
under the gray sea he had spied, as a growth from the floor,
a land to foster multitudes, kindly to sheep.

Straightway he bade Lachesis of the golden veil
lift up her hands, nor deny
the gods' great oath
but assent with the son of Kronos, bending her head; the island
   rising thereafter
into the bright air should be his. The words' end was
   accomplished
with a true fall. Out of the winding water the island

blossomed, held of the father of searing sun-rays,
master of horses that breathe fire. Rhodes mixed with him bore
seven sons, that displayed the shrewdest wits of the men of old
   time.
Of these, one sired Kamiros,
Ialysos, eldest born, and Lindos; sundered, they held

the land of their patrimony in triple division,
each a city, and these are called by their names.

There, as sweet deliverance after the bitterness of misfortune,
to Tlepolemos, Tirynthian arch-founder, is given
as to a god
the smoking processional of sheep, the judgment of games, in
    whose flowers
Diagoras was wreathed twice. At the glorious Isthmos the luck
    four times was his.
One win to crown another at Nemea, at rocky Athens.

The bronze at Argos knew him, the caldrons
in Arkadia and Thebes, the temperate games
Boiotians keep;
Pellana likewise. At Aigina he won six times, at Megara the
    stone ballot
tells no alternate story. But Zeus father, brooding over
the peaks of Atabyrios, honor the set of the song Olympian-ician,

the man who has found excellence with his fists. Grant him
    pleasure of veneration
in the sight of citizens and strangers his friends. The path
    estranged from violence
he walks straitly, sure of all that the upright minds of his
    fathers
left, his heritage. Founder not the seed
of Kallianax, your own. With good fortune for the Eratidai
    the city
has also its part of happiness. But in one parcel of time
the winds intershifting flare to new directions.

Olympia 11

PINDAR

Translated from the Greek by Richmond Lattimore

There is a time when men need most favoring
gales; there is a time for water from the sky,
rain, child of cloud.
But if any endeavor a man win fairly, soft-spoken songs
are given, to be a beginning of men's
speech to come and a true seal on great achievements.

Abundant is such praise laid up for victories
Olympian. My lips have good will
to marshal these words; yet only
by God's grace does a man blossom in the wise turning of his
      thought.
Son of Archestratos, know
that for the sake, Agesidamos, of your boxing.

I shall enchant in strain of song a glory upon
your olive wreath of gold
and bespeak the race of the West Wind Lokrians.
There acclaim him; I warrant you,
Muses, you will visit no gathering cold to strangers
nor lost to lovely things
but deep to the heart in wisdom, and spearmen also. No thing,
      neither devious fox
nor loud lion, may change the nature born in his blood.

Joe Louis Is the Man

JOE PULLUM

Joe Louis is a battlin' man,
The people think his fame will always stand.
He's the brown bomber of this land,
He's supposed to whop 'most any man. . . .
I said Joe is the battlin' man,
Bought his mother a brand new home and some brand new land.
You can gather his intentions must be good,
'Cause he's doing the things for his mother a boy really should.
He's makin' real good money and it doesn't swell his head,
He throws his fist like a 45 throwin' lead.
He throws them heavy and he throws them slow,
Then you know it's powerful Joe,
And boy if he hits you, you sure bound to hit the floor.

Petite Kid Everett

ISHMAEL REED

The bantamweight King of
Newark
He couldn't box
He couldn't dance
He just kept coming at
you, glass chin first
Taking five punches for
every one he connected with
you

Petite Kid Everett
He missed a lot
Slipped a lot and
By mid-life he'd
developed one heck
of a sore head
Took to fighting in
the alley
Gave up wearing a mouthpiece
Beat up his trainers
Beat up the referee
Beat up his fans
Beat up everybody who was
in his corner
Even jumped on Houston Jr.
the lame pail boy
Who didn't have good sense

Petite Kid Everett
There's talk of a comeback
He's got new backers
He stands on one of the four

corners, near the Prudential Life
Building
Trading blow with ghosts
Don't it make you wanna cry?

White Hope

ISHMAEL REED

for shane stevens

jack johnson licked
one pug, so, d man
retired to a farm.
never again opened
his mouth save to
talk abt peachtrees
sow & last year's
almanac:

and whenever somebody
say jack johnson,

he'd get that far away
look.

None but Himself Can Be His Parallel

To Jack Randall the "Nonpareil"

With marble-colored shoulders and keen eyes
Protected by a forehead broad and white,
And hair cut close lest it impede the sight,
And clenched hands, firm, and of punishing size,
Steadily held, or motion'd wary-wise,
To fit or stop—and 'kerchief drawn too tight
O'er the unyielding loins to keep from flight
The inconstant wind that all too often flies—
The Nonpareil stands. Fame whose bright eyes run o'er
With joy to see a chicken of her own,
Dips her rich pen in 'claret' and writes down
Under the letter 'R', first on the score,
'Randall, John—Irish parents—age not known—
Good with both hands, and only ten stone four.'

No, No

YANNIS RITSOS

Translated from the Greek by Scott King

These beautiful heroic (slightly naive, it's true—though still beautiful)
immense white stones and hammers, and those being undressed
in the workshops (mostly muscular wrestlers, boxers)
in imitation of the deeds of others,—one arm raised emphatically,
legs apart in exaggerated balance. No, no—he said—
it's not to be laughed at, and it goes far beyond sorrow;
that mangy dog, covered with ticks and scabs,
drinking dirty water out of the wash bucket
at the base of the half-finished statues of dead heroes.

Dead Shepherd's Hut

DON SCHOFIELD

Sure, I can fix the broken door, clear the brush
out front, find a rope and bucket for the well,
a mattress for the iron bed in this hut
I've rented for next to nothing, but what about
his coat and crook still hanging by the mirror,
the photo of bare-breasted women
in white shorts and red boxing gloves
squared-off and whaling at each other?

I've come here, a tangle of desires,
more like the brambles I open the shutters to, the random
twisted olive trees up this valley kilometers from the road,
come to lose myself in the deep lull
of summer, to be less than smoke
curling from a lamp, nothing and nowhere. I like to think

he woke early, herded the huddled goats
up the ridge, that he knew each one by its bell,
that he's still sitting where pine cones
crack in late morning heat, the place
he slipped through to death. He's buried
on the opposite slope, in the one bare patch
among briars and burned grass—*beyond desire,*

I whisper to myself. But when I stand at his rusty basin,
see these women he gazed at every morning,
the smell of leather and sweat implied
by their gleaming shoulders and gloves, the ripple across one
    breast
where a punch just landed, the spectators cheering
from the darkness surrounding the ring, even the referee
smiling and pointing—I wonder

what he thinks of pleasure now
that he's gone to the source. Dead shepherd,
are you still hovering near your body, or here with me,
gazing at this primal destruction, resenting
even your own birth, that wound that bore you?
Or have you come back with some different knowledge—
taking down your coat and crook
then winking at me with the eyes of a goat, behind their bright
   slits
some truth I just can't see.

Steel Chin

PETER SERCHUK

George Chuvalo was a punching bag;
face full of blood, spitting out teeth.
A tough kid scraped off the Toronto streets,
he sparred with the wind and the cops and the thugs.
He ate in the church with the beggars and nuns
and learned crowds never stay once a man hits the ground.
No matter the punch, no matter the round,
George Chuvalo never went down.
The best fighters in the world reconfigured his face.
Hockey's for punks, he liked to say.

The Boxer

PAUL SIMON

I am just a poor boy
Though my story's seldom told
I have squandered my resistance
For a pocketful of mumbles
Such are promises
All lies and jest
Still a man hears what he wants to hear
And disregards the rest

When I left my home
And my family
I was no more than a boy
In the company of strangers
In the quiet of the railway station
Running scared
Laying low
Seeking out the poorer quarters
Where the ragged people go
Looking for the places
Only they would know

Asking only workman's wages
I come looking for a job
But I get no offers
Just a come-on from the whores on Seventh Avenue
I do declare
There were times when I was so lonesome
I took some comfort there

Now the years are rolling by me
They are rocking evenly
I am older than I once was
Younger than I'll be

But that's not unusual
No it isn't strange
After changes upon changes
We are more or less the same
After changes we are more or less the same

Then I'm laying out my winter clothes
And wishing I was gone
Going home
Where the New York City winters
Aren't bleeding me
Leading me
Going home

In the clearing stands a boxer
And a fighter by his trade
And he carries the reminders
Of ev'ry glove that laid him down
Or cut him till he cried out
In his anger and his shame
"I am leaving, I am leaving"
But the fighter still remains

Closed-Head Wounds

JEFFREY SKINNER

The boxer retires, buys himself a house
in the mountains, red with black shutters. He still gets up
to jog the dirt road early, though not so early
as before, not so fast. Flowers among the weeds
banking the road on either side may be the flowers
of weeds, he doesn't know. Tiny yellow, white,
orange, and one so harshly violet it hurts the eye—
his favorite. He must buy a book of names.
Townspeople are curt without malice, they answer
questions, they make change while turning
back to local friends. Why? Maybe it comes
from living in mountains, he thinks, every horizon
like a muscled back, and who could strut or brag
like homeboys when each morning you drive to work
through *that?* Because some woman told him to,
he has hung suet outside his bedroom window.
When he wakes sometimes half-dreaming
a hummingbird whisks in, like a left hook, stops
short and drinks. He watches, propped on an elbow.
Birds remind him of fast hands, back when he
was no opponent, but took the number-two guy
twelve rounds and almost won. Should have. *Did,* many
said—and not just handlers. The air here like water,
the water like air; cold gusts off the mountains
you inhale against thirst. It's perfect for training,
he catches himself thinking. But that's gone. Ah,
too much has been knocked from his head:
the way feet move against a left-hander, words,
music, sons, women, years. He towels off,
inspects his face in the bathroom mirror, the old
kind: wooden box with mirrored door, screwed to the wall.
Clown ears, wide nose, scars like troughs dug deep
into each brow. *So this is the life,* he thinks, *the rest
of it . . .* And the creature in the box grins back.

Knockout

JOHN SKOYLES

Sometimes two people together
cancel each other out,
and are left dizzy and alone,
as if hesitating outside an office door
where they might not be wanted.
Those seconds are so conspicuous,
slower than the whole long day,
just like that instant in a slow round
when a good left connects,
and the crowd so silent
before it sinks in
that even the aggressor takes a while
to follow it up. And who knows,
his opponent might want to be alone now,
now that the boredom of vertical life has tasted him,
pulling him down like a lover
the way God floored St. Teresa
so she woke up not recognizing anyone,
but content she went through
something glorious and came out even.

Men Versus Men

JOHN SKOYLES

December 20, 1963

This was before much talk of a third world,
and blacks and immigrants wore away
shovelful by shovelful
as the city grew taller.
I was in bed with my father,
pillows propped up,
watching the Friday-night fights,
and Gillette's cartoon parrot
flash the rounds
on a giant safety razor.
Twenty-two years later,
a small piece in the *Times*
recalls the knockout:
2 minutes and 13 seconds,
a precise mathematical notation
hidden in the slop and sweat
of a forgotten life.
For the two faces
staring diagonally
across a canvas mat,
it was business as usual:
both black, one maligned for killing
an opponent in the ring,
the other later serving time.
I like knowing where I was that night,
it made me live over again
an age when I thought of nothing
but men versus men.
Back there,
my father and I praised
the jazzed-up anthem
aimed at the rafters,

and afterward,
the deft, almost archeological
effort to coax a man back
from his twitching oblivion.

Sonny Liston

JOHN SKOYLES

He saw it in his father's eyes;
he drank it from his mother,
and most of his life he tried
to keep it out of places
where other people noticed it.
If it showed on his face,
he smiled, and made a joke of it.

So what if everyone laughed
and went along with it,
because he found a sport
that almost taunted it,
but each night lying in the dark
he confessed he was afraid of it,
and the shadow boxing in the hall
boxed on, suspecting it.

Alphabet for the Fancy

CHARLES SLOMAN

A   stands for *Aaron* who fought for the prize,
B   for *Big Brown,* who's afraid of his eyes;
C   is for *Curtis,* the *Fancy's* own Pet,
D   for *Dick Davis,* on whom many bet;
E   is for Egan, the pride of the Ring,
     His Life in London's the out-and-out thing;
F   is for *Fogo,* the Ring's natty poet,
G   stands for *Gas,* who good fighting can show it;
H   is for *Hudson,* the famed John Bull fighter,
I   is for *Inglis,* no lad e'er was tighter;
J   is for *Jones,* the Sailor Boy true,
K   is for *Kirkman,* who's always true blue;
L   is for *Lenney,* the Cow Boy of fame,
M   was for *Martin,* who always was game;
N   is for *Neate,* who once fought with Tom Spring,
O   is for *Oliver,* once of the Ring;
P   was for *Painter,* a fighter so bold,
Q   is for *Queering,* when battles are sold;
R   is for *Randall,* the famed Nonpareil,
S   is for *Savage,* who makes his blows tell;
T   was for *Turner,* whom Randall oft beat,
U   is the *Umpire,* whom fighters all greet;
V   is for *Venture,* the money that's bet,
W   for *Ward,* who his man always met;
X   stands for *Cross,* which the *Fancy* decry,
     "No go!" was the *chaunt*—and now it's gone by.
Y   is for *Yokels,* who're always down brown,
Z   in the record I will not put down.

Confessions of a Licensed Professional Boxing Judge

CLAUDE CLAYTON SMITH

I perch high on my stool
in no-man's-land
(though women now fight
on every card),
a neutral presence
between the apron
and most expensive seats:
right where the ring girl
swings her leg up, then
splits the ropes
to strut her stuff.

I pray for knockouts:
they make my job easy.
Or knockdowns,
which mean a ten–eight round.
The even rounds are tough:
no edge or advantage, no telling
jab or body-shot, no counter-punch.
The Commissioner frowns
when we mark our sheets ten–ten.

I pray the local boy wins, though
I've sent many home unhappy,
deaf-and-dumb to screaming
family and friends.
I never squirm
unless the fight goes the distance.
No one likes a draw,
a split decision. In my head,
a running tally of blows.

Blues for Benny "Kid" Paret

DAVE SMITH

For years I've watched the corners for signs.
A hook, a jab, a feint, the peekaboo prayer of forearms,
anything for the opening, the rematch I go on dreaming.
What moves can say your life is saved?

    As I backpedaled in a field the wasps' nest waited,
    playing another game: a child peeps out of
    my eyes now, confused by a rage of stinging,
    wave after wave rising as I tell my fists to hurt me,
    hurt the pain. I take my own beating, God help me

    it hurts. Everything hurts, every punch darts,
    jolts, enters my ears, bangs my temples. Who hurts
    a man faster than himself? There was a wall I
    bounced on, better than ropes. I was eleven years old.

In that year I saw the fog
turn aside and rise from the welts you were
to run away with its cousin the moon. They smacked
your chest and crossed your arms because you fell down
while the aisles filled with gorgeous women, high heels
pounding off like Emile, the Champion, who planted
his good two feet and stuck, stuck, stuck, stuck
until your brain tied up your tongue and your breath.

    Somebody please, please I cried,
    make them go away, but the ball in my hand was
    feverish with the crackling light. I could not let go
    as I broke against the wall. I was eleven years old.

Benny Paret, this night in a car ferrying
my load of darkness like a ring no one escapes,

I am bobbing and weaving in fog split only by a radio
whose harsh gargle is eleven years old, a voice in the air

telling the night you're down, counting time,
and I hear other voices, corners with bad moves
say *Get up you son of a bitch, get up and fight!* But you don't
get up again in my life and the only life you had is gone

with the moon I remember sailing down on your heart
where you lay in blood, waiting, photo flashes all snapped,
eyes open to take whatever is yet to come, jabs, hooks, cross
breaking through the best prayer you ever lifted to dump
you dizzied and dreamless in the green soft grass.

Championship Fight

DAVE SMITH

The big Plymouth shuddered with all the speed
it could give us, jammed by my father's
planted right foot. We wallowed through days
and nights, struck at the feints of curves,
bobbing and weaving, shooting in and out
of neighborhoods long dark as old sweats.
We liked the smoky rooms, the night's smells
that heaved us right and left, then back
so we seemed always to be rolling on shocks
belly-soft. That wheezy hulk wouldn't quit.

My sister and I learned how to laugh, bounced
over the fabric that still prickles my face.
We were quick and capable of anything then,
little faces darting in that tub of darkness,
howling until once again we were stopped
inside the float of dust that rose up to say
like a bodiless voice Ladies and Gentleman,
arrived all the way from. . . . Wherever. Now

I don't know, I can't remember who it was
my father had come to fight, why it mattered,
only that he leaps from the car onto rocks,
instantly slinks into the shape of Marciano,
whom he loved, no one man enough anywhere
to take down the Brockton Bomber and live.
Yet I saw that black fighter make the spit
lick from that broken mouth before the bar
emptied its first row of booths. It was fast.

Wherever we went after that, my mother's gaze
glared back at the moon cool on the windshield.
His knockout, he called her. Driving at all

the things we never saw ahead, he'd reach
back for us, grabbing arm or leg, and squeeze
until the fat car rocked, and left us grinning.
I never thought this would be what I'd remember
when I had curled into the black corner, not
sleeping, afraid. I thought it would be him
crying, drooling blood into a stranger's ditch,
who said Jesus, oh Jesus, it's over so quick.

Muhammad Ali at Ringside, 1985

WOLE SOYINKA

The arena is darkened. A feast of blood
Will follow duly; the spotlights have been borrowed
For a while. These ringside prances
Merely serve to whet the appetite. Gladiators,
Clad tonight in formal mufti, customised,
Milk recognition, savour the night-off, show-off
Rites. Ill fitted in this voyeur company,
The desperate arm wrap of the tiring heart
Gives place to social hugs, the slow-count
One to ten to a snappy "Give-me-five!"
Toothpaste grins replace the death-mask
Rubber gumshield grimaces. Promiscuous
Peck-a-cheek supplants the maestro's peek-a-boo.

The roped arena waits; an umpire tests the floor,
Tests whiplash boundaries of the rope.
The gallant's exhibition rounds possess
These foreplay moments. Gloves in silk-white sheen
Rout lint and leather. Paco Rabanne rules the air.
A tight-arsed soubriette checks her placard smile
To sign the rounds for blood and gore.

Eased from the navel of Bitch-Mother Fame
A microphone, neck-ruffed silver-filigree—as one
Who would usurp the victor's garland—stabs the air
For instant prophesies. In cosy insulation, bathed
In teleglow, distant homes have built
Their own vicarious rings—the forecast claimed
Four million viewers on the cable deal alone;
Much "bread" was loaded on the scales
At weighing hour—till scores are settled. One
Will leave the fickle womb tonight
Smeared in combat fluids, a broken fetus.

The other, toned in fire, a dogged phoenix
Oblivious of the slow countdown of inner hurts
Will thrust his leaden fists in air
Night prince of the world of dreams.

One sits still. His silence is a dying count.
At last the lens acknowledges the tested
Hulk that dominates, even in repose
The giddy rounds of furs and diamond pins.
A brief salute—the camera is kind,
Discreetly pans, and masks the doubletalk
Of medicine-men—"Has the syndrome
But not the consequence." Promoters, handlers
It's time to throw in the towel—Parkinson's
Polysyllables have failed to tease a rhyme
From the once nimble Louisville Lips.

The camera flees, distressed. But not before
The fire of battle flashes in those eyes
Rekindled by the moment's urge to centerstage.
He rules the night space even now, bestrides
The treacherous domain with thighs of bronze,
A dancing mural of delights. Oh Ali! Ale-e-e . . .

What music hurts the massive head tonight, Ali!
The drums, the tin cans, the guitars and *mbira* of Zaire?
Aa-lee! Aa-lee! Aa-lee *Bomaye! Bomaye!*
The Rumble in the Jungle? Beauty and the Beast?
Roll call of Bum-a-Month. The rope-a-dope?
The Thrilla in Manila?—Ah-lee! Ah-lee!
"The closest thing to death," you said. Was that
The greatest, saddest prophesy of all? Oh, Ali!

Black tarantula whose antics hypnotize the foe!
Butterfly side slipping death from rocket probes.
Bee whose sting, unsheathed, picks the teeth
Of the raging hippopotamus, then fans
The jaw's convergence with its flighty wings.

Needle that threads the snapping fangs
Of crocodiles, knots the tusks of elephants
On rampage. Cricket that claps and chirrups
Round the flailing horn of the rhinoceros,
Then shuffles, does a bugalloo, tap-dances on its tip.
Space that yields, then drowns the intruder
In showers of sparks—oh Ali! Ali!
Esu with faces turned to all four compass points,
Astride a weather vane; they sought to trap him,
Slapped the wind each time. He brings a message—
All know the messenger, the neighborhood is roused—
Yet no one sees his face, he waits for no reply,
Only that combination three-four calling card,
The wasp-tail legend: I've been there and gone.
Mortar that goads the pestle: Do you call that
Pounding? The yam is not yet smooth—
Pound, dope, pound! When I have eaten the yam,
I'll chew the fiber that once called itself
A pestle! Warrior who said, "I will not fight,"
Yet proved a prophet's call to arms against a war.

Cassius Marcellus, Warrior, Muhammad Prophet,
Flesh is clay, all, all too brittle mould.
The bout is over. Frayed and split and autographed,
The gloves are hung up in the Hall of Fame—
Still loaded, even from that first blaze of gold
And glory. Awed multitudes will gaze,
New questers feast on these mementos
And from their shell-shocked remnants
Reinvoke the spell. But the sorcerer is gone,
The lion withdrawn to a lair of time and space
Inaccessible as the sacred lining of a crown
When kings were kings, and lords of rhyme and pace.
The enchantment is over but the spell remains.

Joe Louis

DAVID SPICER

The last time I saw Joe Louis
he sat in a wheelchair at a stadium.
I kept glancing at this old man
boxed in by loneliness,
children and money gone.
Sometimes he'd look up
when he heard the crack of the bat
and wait for the ball to land at his feet.
He hadn't had luck like that in years, I guessed,
recalling how the only person
he wanted to kill was Schmeling.
I stared at the Brown Bomber,
who seemed to own sadness:
When I was a sailor on the *USS Washington,*
I went up against him
with no chance of slipping in one punch.
Quicker than a thief escaping an angel's grasp,
he flicked jabs at my chin,
and I bobbed back,
stunned but glorious in defeat.
After the men carried me out,
I heard the legs dancing above
and ran up the ship's ladder to see
sailor after sailor lying on stretchers
like explosion victims.
Nobody could uppercut or left hook him
before he one-twoed them,
and they landed on deck
with a thud louder than the 16-inch-gun's blast.
Twenty of the ship's toughest swabbies
traded punches with the man that day—
officers, cooks, beerbellies, weightlifters—
and nobody aboard worried about the Japs or God.

Those few hours two thousand of us watched
and fought Joe Louis,
who pedalled across the ring to home in
on the opponent before he floored him
with a steamhammer punch.
The fighters fell face first,
and the lowest seamen threw buckets
of cold saltwater on the bloody canvas to our cheers.
We wanted a shipmate to win, but only one lasted
more than three rounds with Joe Louis: in the fourth
a fast Italian named Monzoni slugged toe to toe,
which was a mistake—
he fell harder than anyone.
We knew Joe Louis didn't want to hurt us,
a genius so gifted he couldn't escape
until age knocked him out of the ring.
I knew this the day I saw him
in the giant bowl, where men tested strength
and skills as they had for centuries.
I wanted to march up to the champion
gazing up at the sky like a condemned senator
and kiss him with humility I couldn't muster.
But I realized that fallen heroes
require more than adulation:
at this moment the broadcaster shouted through
the public announcement system and seventy
thousand bodies stared at the figure behind me,
stood up and applauded for ten minutes
the man who just nodded, bowed and nodded
his head again to a city of sport fans
that felt the same way I did.

Monster

DAVID STEINGASS

I aim for the tip of the nose to drive the bone into the brain.
—Mike Tyson

Scorpions under the skin
At his shoulders and back scribbled
Code on the walls of our sleep.
Still he flexed and jabbed
Until we felt the chairs we sat in
Move, until the light
Glaring in his sweat dazed
Each smoky eye into fangs.

We watched our pulses bang
Their tiny gates as we wrenched
Away from the ritual
Of his rage, children
Grown skeletal at the open
Grave we stared into
Unconvinced as we washed
And washed the blood again
From our hands.

Cuban Bon Bon

VIRGIL SUÁREZ

for Eligio Sardinius-Montalbo,
a.k.a Kid Chocolate
Featherweight champion 1932–1933
Jr. lightweight champion 1931–1933
Record: 132–10–6 (50 K.O.'s)

He learned to throw anvil-hard punches
    from watching films of other boxers,
    the hammer-left from Joe Gans, that slippery
right from Benny Leonard, and deathblow uppercut
    from Jack Johnson. If you asked his
    opponents—good boxers like Fidel LaBarba,
Al Singer, and Bushy Graham—they'd say
    Kid Chocolate always drew close enough
    to whisper a Cuban tune in your ears,
while his hands buzzed before your face,
    and *Dios Mio* if one punch landed
    on your temple, or jaw, then the world
would spin, you'd hear the thunder
    a boulder makes tumbling down a mountainside . . .
    In New York, he partied for days on end,
blondes his weakness, *las rubias,* as he called
    these ladies of fair, supple skin, *suavecitas*
    like flour, and the scent of jasmine water
on their flesh, that softest part of their thighs.
    Those were the days, he thinks as an old
    and retired boxer in Cuba, the tropical sun
hot on his scalp, his memory of taking down
    Benny "The Fish" Bass in Philadelphia
    for the world title, and he did it in rare form.
Then came Tony Canzoneri who KOed him
    in the second round, and Freddie Klick who
    stripped him of his Jr. Lightweight title . . .
And it's like being on a downward slope

in one of those Oriente province hills, a kid
and he's coming down on a bicycle, hard
and fast, letting go of the steering wheel,
  the wind catching in your mouth, choking
  time and memory into one giant gulp-sound
of surrender . . . the *bon bon* meant a lot
  for the ladies who held him in New York,
  Philly, Boston, in all those strange cities
he fought and won, found and lost, *bomb-
  bomb* his opponents thought the *bon-bon*
  meant, but it was the smooth silk of cocoa,
the way his hands came at you like a sudden
  Cuban rainstorm, out of nowhere,
  and then you looked up and saw a flash of light,
huge tropical drops daggering down, knocking you blind.

Poetry Reading

WISŁAWA SZYMBORSKA

Translated from the Polish by Stanisław Barańczak and Clare Cavanagh

To be a boxer, or not to be there
at all. O Muse, where are *our* teeming crowds?
Twelve people in the room, eight seats to spare—
it's time to start this cultural affair.
Half came inside because it started raining,
the rest are relatives. O Muse.

The women here would love to rant and rave,
but that's for boxing. Here they must behave.
Dante's Inferno is ringside nowadays.
Likewise his Paradise. O Muse.

Oh, not to be a boxer but a poet,
one sentenced to hard shelleying for life,
for lack of muscles forced to show the world
the sonnet that may make the high-school reading lists
with luck. O Muse,
O bobtailed angel, Pegasus.

In the first row, a sweet old man's soft snore:
he dreams his wife's alive again. What's more,
she's making him that tart she used to bake.
Aflame, but carefully—don't burn his cake!—
we start to read. O Muse.

Shadowboxing

JAMES TATE

Sometimes you almost get a punch in.
Then you may go for days without even seeing him,
or his presence may become a comfort
for a while.

He says: I saw you scrambling last night
on your knees and hands.

He says: How come you always want to be
something else, how come you never take your life
seriously?

And you say: Shut up! Isn't it enough
I say I love you, I give you everything!

He moves across the room with his hand
on his chin, and says: How great you are!

Come here, let me touch you, you say.

He comes closer. Come closer, you say.
He comes closer. Then. *Whack!* And
you start again, moving around and around
the room, the room which grows larger
and larger, darker and darker. The black moon.

The Fight of Sayerius and Heenanus
A Lay of Ancient London

WILLIAM MAKEPEACE THACKERAY

(Supposed to be recounted to his great-grandchildren, 17 April, A.D. 1920,
by an Ancient Gladiator)

. . . What know ye, race of milksops
    Untaught of the P.R.,
What stepping, lunging, countering,
    Fibbing or rallying are?
What boots to use the lingo,
    When you have not the thing?
How paint to you the glories
    Of Belcher, Cribb or Spring—
To you, whose sire turns up his eyes
    At mention of the Ring?

Then each his hand stretched forth to grasp,
His foeman's fives in friendly clasp;
Each felt his balance trim and true—
Each up to square his mauleys threw;
Each tried his best to draw his man—
The feint, the dodge, the opening plan,
Till left and right Sayerius tried;
Heenanus' grin proclaimed him wide;
He shook his nut, a lead essayed,
Nor reached Sayerius' watchful head.
At length each left is sudden flung;
We heard the pondcrous thud,
And from each tongue the news was wrung,
Sayerius hath "First Blood".

Adown Heenanus' Roman nose,
Freely the tell-tale claret flows,

While stern Sayerius' forehead shows
That in the interchange of blows,
Heenanus' aim was good.
Again each iron mauley swung,
And loud the counter hitting rung,
Till breathless all, and wild with blows,
Fiercely they grapple for the close;
A moment in close hug they swing,
Hither and thither around the ring,
Then from Heenanus' clinch of brass
Sayerius smiling slips to grass.

I trow mine ancient breath would fail,
    To follow through the fight
Each gallant round's still changing tale,
    Each feat of left and right;
How through two well-fought hours and more
    Through bruise, and blow, and blood,
Like sturdy bulldogs as they were,
    Those well-matched heroes stood;

How nine times in that desperate mill,
    Heenanus in his strength,
Knocked about Sayerius off his pins,
    And laid him all at length;
But how in each succeeding round,
    Sayerius smiling came,
With head as cool and wind as sound,
    As his first moment on the ground,
Still confident and game,
    How from Heenanus' sledge-like fist,
Striving a smasher to resist.

Sayerius' stout right arm gave way,
Yet the maimed hero still made play,
And when "in-fighting" threatened ill,
Was nimble in "out-fighting" still—

Still did his own maintain,
In mourning put Heenanus' glims,
Till blinded eyes and helpless limbs,
    He chances squared again.
How blind Heenanus, in despite
Of bleeding face and waning sight,
So gallantly kept up the fight,
    That not a man could say
Which of the two 'twere wise to back,
Or on which side some random crack
    Might not decide the day;
And leave us—whoso won the prize—
Victor and vanquished, in all eyes,
    An equal need to pay.

Two hours and more the fight had sped,
    Near unto ten it drew,
But still opposed one-armed to blind,
    They stood those dauntless two.
Ah, me! That I have lived to hear
    Such men as ruffians scorned,
Such deeds of valour "brutal" called,
    Canted, preached down, and mourned!
Ah! that these old eyes ne'er again
    A gallant mill shall see!
No more behold the ropes and stakes,
    With colours flying free!

But I forgot the combat—
    How shall I tell the close?
That left the Champion's belt in doubt
    Between those well-matched foes!
Fain would I shroud the tale in night—
The meddling Blues that thrust in sight—
    The ring-keepers o'er thrown—
The broken ropes—th' encumbered fight—
Heenanus' sudden blinded flight—

Sayerius pausing, as he might,
Just when ten minutes, used aright,
    Had made the day his own!

Alas e'en in those bright days
    We still had Beaks and Blues;
Still canting rogues their mud to fling,
On self-defense and on the ring,
    And fistic art abuse.
And 'twas such varmint had the power,
    The Champions' fight to stay,
And leave unsettled to this hour
    The honours of that day.
But had those honours rested—
    Divided, as was due—
Sayerius and Heenanus
    Had cut the belt in two.

And now my fists are feeble,
    And my blood is thin and cold,
But 'tis better than Old Tom to me,
    To recall those days of old.
And may you, my great grandchildren,
    That gather round my knee,
Ne'er see worse men nor iller times
    Than I and mine might be,
Thought England then had prize-fighters—
    Even reprobates like me.'

The Gym on Tchoupitoulas Street

ERIC TRETHEWEY

Evenings, we came from the corners
of the city, between office buildings
lit-up for cleaners and sweepers,
to the warehouse gym by the river,
boys and men hungry for proof
that hands and heart are enough
to bang big-chested dreams
into something to be lived—
we came through the alley,
upstairs past posters telling our trade,
and entered the hollow of the dinging bell
measuring motion from lights-on to lights-out
(one minute, three minutes, one minute),
old men with pasts hammered into their faces,
and the rest of us, tattooed, broken-toothed,
bearing our salt-stained gear, our records,
our woofing "make-his-ass-wide" talk—
we came to jab and rip hooks
at bags and bodies,
or dance away from darkness
wrapped up tight into fists—
the one who fought for the title,
then hung around to prove to us
that what an ice pick in the head
and the best middleweights in the world
couldn't do, cheap wine could,
and the other, sparring for a bout
slated years too late to matter,
who left his fight and his corpse
in the gym, the bleeders, the breakers,
the ones who could hit like mules
but had hearts like peas, and those
who couldn't break an egg who had hearts

that wouldn't quit, couldn't quit,
had fight in them like shit has stink,
all of us trading blood, teeth, brains
to rise out of our lives,
crack the ratings, fight
for the title, some of us did,
none of us ever won.

In the Louisiana State Prison at Angola

ERIC TRETHEWEY

"I was just a lot of front street action,"
he says, humbled by concrete and metal,
arguments no sane man can resist,
as he tries to recall the battles,
the pay days, the mellow nights he knows
are as bright now without him
as they were before this new sentence
of life without illusions began
to stalk his every shift and weave.
Enlarged by foreshortening,
his big-knuckled hands dangle
through the bars, flesh on steel,
in the photo that leaps out
from the scrambled Sunday news
to take me back across the years
and into the gyms where long ago
we trained for mayhem
that is less now than memory.

He looks older, balding, his face lined,
flesh settled down in its sag along the bone,
and with the picture and these words
I sicken into an old sense
of what has always been wrong
with this world of bitter risings
into dawn. The record shows
he has twice slashed his wrists,
and once, sitting on his bunk,
eyes upraised to the dark ceiling of the cell,
he poured laundry bleach
down into their funneled light
to drown out the wars of wolves on punks,

and teach himself to live
on less than hope's willed fiction.

The past that is tattooed on his body
is best forgotten: scars from the ring,
the names of a wife, children
who have moved on to other lives.
This is nothing but the way things are.
The story before me is called justice
by some, but there is nothing
of value to be learned here,
except what a man may utter
from a place justice has never been.

"My hook stinks now," he says, "but goddam,
other fighters keep themselves mad—
I couldn't keep myself mad,"
forty years having shown him at last
that he couldn't have lived without anger,
and that justice in the world he's known
is nothing more than raging grace—
that smoldered in him in the dawn
and gutters now for air to flame out fierce
against this savage cage of night.

Amateur Fighter

NATASHA TRETHEWEY

for my father

What's left is the tiny gold glove
hanging from his key chain. But,
before that, he had come to boxing,

as a boy, out of necessity—one more reason
to stay away from home, go late
to that cold house and dinner alone

in the dim kitchen. Perhaps he learned
just to box a stepfather, then turned
that anger into a prize at the Halifax gym.

Later, in New Orleans, there were the books
he couldn't stop reading. A scholar, his eyes
weakening. Fighting, then, a way to live

dangerously. He'd leave his front tooth out
for pictures so that I might understand
living meant suffering, loss. Really living

meant taking risks, so he swallowed
a cockroach in a bar on a dare, dreamt
of being a bullfighter. And at the gym

on Tchoupitoulas Street, he trained
his fists to pound into a bag
the fury contained in his gentle hands.

The red headgear, hiding his face,
could make me think he was someone else,
that my father was somewhere else, not here

holding his body up to pain.

Liston

WILLIAM TROWBRIDGE

In an allegory, he'd have been Brute Force?
hulking frame, liver lips, blunt stare assessive
as a prowling shark's. "Everybody's bad Nigger,"

smirked the *Esquire* title underneath the close-up
of a countenance imposing as a fifth face
on Mount Rushmore, sweat-beaded blowup

of what you might glimpse just before
an eighteen-wheeler barreled through you.
Everybody's heavyweight stripped down

to the raw essentials: bone and muscle, rage
and felonies; black trunks with white stripes,
blackout with twinkly stars. We loved the chill

he gave us, our glowering pit bull we sicced
on all contenders, our looming shadow,
our two-time loser from Castle Frankenstein,

until the "phantom punch," when he sat down
wobbly as a dowager, leaving the floor
to the lippy punk from Louisville. We felt

betrayed, diminished, tongue tied by that
prattling dancer with the couplets and pretty face.
We wanted blood, teeth. Nothing fancy.

Queer Street

WILLIAM TROWBRIDGE

is where they said LaMotta got waylaid
when he stopped that uppercut from Sugar Ray
and kept on standing, or where Basilio wandered
when, once more, his delicate eyes puffed
into two large eggs cooked over easy. It's there
we find ourselves when the playground bully
springs our clock or the green-gowned medico
says breathe deep and count to ten. By five
it's Queer Street, that titled byway
through Palookaville, that rambling road
between this world and the next, which doesn't
look as if it leads to anywhere important,
bliss or opposite. Its few dim bulbs
flicker behind the copper-tasting haze,
and there we stand, befuddled and alone, feeling
more like the village idiot than a traveler
with one foot in the absolute. Quite disappointing,
really, if we had the sense to think so.

*

From *The Aeneid:* The Boxing Match

VIRGIL

Translated from the Latin by Rolfe Humphries

They take their stand, each rising
On the balls of his feet, their arms upraised, and rolling
Their heads back from the punch. They spar, they lead,
They watch for openings. Dares, much the younger,
Is much the better in footwork; old Entellus
Has to rely on strength; his knees are shaky,
His wind not what it was. They throw their punches,
And many miss; and some, with a solid thump,
Land on the ribs or chest; temples and ears
Feel the wind of a miss, or the jaws rattle
When a punch lands. Entellus stands flat-footed,
Wasting no motion, just a slip of the body,
The watchful eyes alert. And Dares, feinting,
Like one who artfully attacks a city,
Tries this approach, then that, dancing around him
In varied vain attack. Entellus, rising,
Draws back his right (in fact, he telegraphs it),
And Dares, seeing it coming, slips aside;
Entellus lands on nothing but the wind
And, thrown off balance, heavily comes down
Flat on his face, as falls on Erymanthus
A thunder-smitten oak, and so on, and so on.
Roaring, the Trojans and Sicilians both
Rise to their feet; the noise goes up to heaven;
Acestes rushes in, to raise his comrade
In pity and sorrow. But that old-time fighter
Is not slowed down a bit, nor made more wary;
His rage is terrible, and his shame awakens
A consciousness of strength. He chases Dares
All over the ring, left, right, left, right, the punches
Rattle like hailstones on a roof; he batters Dares,

Spins him halfway around with one hand, clouts him
Straight with the other again. At last Aeneas
Steps in and stops it, with a word of comfort
For the exhausted Dares.

Punch-Drunk

MICHAEL WATERS

It's when the brains get shook up and run together that you get punch-drunk.
     —Sonny Liston

Tough guys swayed with Archie Moore
when his legs began to go,
that heavy surf slowing
the late rounds, each jab

blurring the ropes, the lights
liquid, his body begging
to drift with dignity down.
No easy thing to quit the ring.

When I faced a former lover
in Rockefeller Center, crowds hushed
as if a left hook had connected,
so I blinked through water,

and almost started to swim
Sixth Avenue in delirium,
before slurring some dumb greeting,
then stumbling toward the corner bar.

I can still see that submerged
corridor, and celebrate Archie Moore,
ex-champ, visiting Stillman's gym,
his world frozen for a moment—

the heavy bags, sparring partners,
the hungry shadows punching walls—
until the contenders resume,
having nodded their respect,

and sweat thaws the silence
that had broken open the air.

Boxing Lesson

CHARLES HARPER WEBB

Don't tense up. Don't cringe away.
If you move back, don't move straight
back. Circle. Circle. Bob and weave.
Feint and roll. Relax. Stay focused.
The more scared you are of getting hit,
the easier to hit you are.
Have fun. Don't sweat it.
It's like sex: stay loose if you want
to punch hard. Make friends with pain.
Know you can take the shock of the left
jab that yanks the right behind,
the uppercut that unhinges your jaw,
the left hook that lifts you out
of consciousness like a fish
out of a wave.

                Exhausted, keep
your breath steady, your jab pumping,
your face hard. Always provide
something to fear. Hurt, never run
or look away. Leap in and hug
your man. Crush his power
to your chest. Make him the post
that keeps you upright. Civilization
means overruling instinct:
embracing the counter-intuitive,
knowing the world, that seems so flat,
will curve if you sail far enough,
that massive hunks of steel can fly,
that staring death straight in the eye
can save your life.

King Joe (Joe Louis Blues)

RICHARD WRIGHT

Black-eyed peas ask cornbread, "What makes you so strong?"
Black-eyes peas ask cornbread, "What makes you so strong?"
Cornbread say, "I come from where Joe Louis was born."

Joe don't talk much, but he talks all the time.
Joe don't talk much, but he talks all the time.
Now you can look at Joe but you sure don't read his mind.

Lord, I know a secret, swore I'd never tell,
Lord, I know a secret, swore I'd never tell.
I know what makes old Joe book and punch and roll like hell.

Rabbit say to bee, what make you sting so deep?
Rabbit say to bee, what make you sting so deep?
Bee say I sting like Joe and rock 'em all to sleep.

They say old Joe just lays down sleeps all day long,
They say old Joe just lays down sleeps all day long,
What old Joe does at night, Lord, sure 'ain't done him no wrong.

Been in Cleveland, St. Louis, and Chicago, too;
Been in Cleveland, St. Louis, and Chicago, too;
But the best is Harlem when a Joe Louis fight is through.

Old Joe wrestled Ford engines, Lord, it was a shame;
Say old Joe hugged Ford engines, Lord, it was a shame;
And he turned engine himself and went to the fighting game.

If you want to see something, just watch Old Joe roll with a
    blow,
If you want to see something, just watch Old Joe roll with a
    blow,
Lord, Lord, bet he didn't learn that trick at no boxing show.

Big Black bearcat couldn't turn nothing loose he caught;
Big Black bearcat couldn't turn nothing loose he caught;
Squeezed it 'til the count of nine, and just couldn't be bought.

Now molasses is black and they say buttermilk is white,
Now molasses is black and they say buttermilk is white,
If you eat a bellyful of both, it's like a Joe Louis fight.

Wonder what Joe Louis thinks when he's fighting a white man,
Say wonder what Joe thinks when he's fighting a white man?
Bet he thinks what I'm thinking, 'cause he wears a deadpan.

Lord, I hate to see old Joe Louis step down,
Lord, I hate to see old Joe Louis step down,
But I bet a million dollars no man will ever wear his crown.

Bullfrog told boll weevil: Joe's done quit the ring,
Bullfrog told boll weevil: Joe's done quit the ring,
Boll weevil say: He ain't gone and he's still the king.

Boom Boom Mancini

WARREN ZEVON

Hurry home early—hurry on home
Boom Boom Mancini's fighting Bobby Chacon
Hurry home early—hurry on home
Boom Boom Mancini's fighting Bobby Chacon

From Youngstown, Ohio, Ray "Boom Boom" Mancini
A lightweight contender, like father like son
He fought for the title with Frias in Vegas
And he put him away in round number one

Hurry home early—hurry on home
Boom Boom Mancini's fighting Bobby Chacon
Hurry home early—hurry on home
Boom Boom Mancini's fighting Bobby Chacon

When Alexis Arguello gave Boom Boom a beating
Seven weeks later he was back in the ring
Some have the speed and the right combinations
If you can't take the punches, it don't mean a thing

Hurry home early—hurry on home
Boom Boom Mancini's fighting Bobby Chacon
Hurry home early—hurry on home
Boom Boom Mancini's fighting Bobby Chacon

When they asked him who was responsible
For the death of Du Koo Kim
He said, "Some one should have stopped the fight
And told me it was him."
They made hypocrite judgments after the fact
But the name of the game is be hit and hit back

Hurry home early—hurry on home
Boom Boom Mancini's fighting Bobby Chacon
Hurry home early—hurry on home
Boom Boom Mancini's fighting Bobby Chacon

Suck It Up

PAUL ZIMMER

Two pugs on the undercard step through
The ropes in satin robes,
Pink Adidas with tassels,
Winking at the women in the crowd.
At instructions they stare down hard
And refuse to touch their gloves,
Trying to make everyone believe
That this will be a serious dust-up.

But when the bell rings they start
Slapping like a couple of Barbie Dolls.
One throws a half-hearted hook,
The other flicks out his jab,
They bounce around for a while
Then grab each other for a tango.
The crowd gets tired of booing
and half of them go out for beer,
But I've got no place to hide.

A week after a cancer scare,
A year from a detached retina,
Asthmatic, overweight, trickling,
Drooling, bent like a blighted elm
In my pajamas and slippers,
I have tuned up my hearing aids to sit in
Numbness without expectation before
These televised Tuesday Night Fights.

With a minute left in the fourth,
Scuffling, they butt their heads
By accident. In midst of all the catcalls
And hubbub suddenly they realize
How much they hate each other.

They start hammering and growling,
Really dealing, whistling combinations,
Hitting on the breaks and thumbing.
At last one guy crosses a stiff jab
With a roundhouse right and the other
Loses his starch. The guy wades into
The wounded one, pounding him
Back and forth until he goes down,
Bouncing his head hard on the canvas.

The count begins but he is saved
By the bell and his trainers haul
Him to his stool as the lens zooms in.

I come to the edge of my La-Z-Boy,
Blinking and groaning from my incision,
Eager for wise, insightful instruction.

He gets a bucket of water in his face,
A sniff on the salts while the cutman
Tries to close his wounds with glue.
His nose is broken, eyes are crossed,
His lips bleed like two rare steaks.
His cornermen take turns slapping his cheeks.
"Suck it up!" they shout.
"Suck it up!"

ACKNOWLEDGMENTS

The editors are most grateful to Tammy Wadley for her generous assistance in the preparation of the manuscript.

"Late Round" copyright © Kim Addonizio. Reprinted from *The Philosopher's Club* by Kim Addonizio (BOA Editions, Ltd., 1994) by permission of the author.

"The Shadowboxer" copyright © 1991 by Ai. Reprinted by permission of the author.

"Narrative: Ali" and "Today's News" copyright © 1994 by Elizabeth Alexander. Reprinted by permission of the author.

"Clay Comes Out to Meet Liston" by Muhammad Ali. Written by Gary Belkin for recitation by Cassius Clay on *I Am the Greatest!* by Cassius Clay, Columbia Records, 1963, 1964. Reprinted by permission of Gary Belkin.

"Fightin' Was Natural" copyright © 1990 by Maya Angelou. Reprinted from *I Shall Not Be Moved* by Maya Angelou by permission of Random House, Inc.

"Epitaph" (anonymous) is reprinted from *The Noble Art,* edited by T. B. Shepherd. London: Hollis and Carter, 1950.

"Hallowed Ground" (anonymous) is reprinted from *The Noble Art,* edited by T. B. Shepherd. London: Hollis and Carter, 1950.

"I Went Down Last Tuesday Night" (anonymous) is reprinted from *Joe Louis: The Great Black Hope,* by Richard Bak. Cambridge, Mass.: Da Capo Press, 1998.

"Parody on Part of Gray's 'Elegy in a Churchyard' " (anonymous) is reprinted from *The Noble Art,* edited by T. B. Shepherd. London: Hollis and Carter, 1950.

"You Valiant Sons of Erin's Isle" (anonymous) is reprinted from *The Noble Art,* edited by T. B. Shepherd. London: Hollis and Carter, 1950.

"A Dream of the Ring: The Great Jack Johnson" copyright © 1994 by George Barlow. Reprinted by permission of the author.

Lyric of "That's What the Well-Dressed Man in Harlem Will Wear" by Irving Berlin. Copyright © 1942 by Irving Berlin. Copyright © renewed by Irving Berlin. International copyright secured. All rights reserved. Reprinted by permission.

"The Boxing Lesson" copyright © 2002 by Richard Broderick. Reprinted by permission of the author.

"Crispus Attucks McKoy" and "Strange Legacies" copyright © 1980 by Sterling A. Brown. Reprinted from *The Collected Poems of Sterling A. Brown,* edited by Michael S. Harper, by permission of HarperCollins Publishers Inc.

"the loser" copyright © 1988 by Charles Bukowski. Reprinted from *The Roominghouse Madrigals: Early Selected Poems 1946–1966* by Charles Bukowski by permission of Black Sparrow Press.

"Owed to Joe Louis" by John Kieran copyright © 1941 by John Kieran and Joseph W. Golinkin. Copyright © renewed 1969 by John Kieran. Reprinted from *The American Sporting Scene* by John Kieran by permission of Scribner, a Division of Simon and Schuster, Inc.

"The House of Blue Light" copyright © 2000 by David Kirby. Reprinted from *The House of Blue Light* by David Kirby by permission of Louisiana State University Press.

"Boxing Day" copyright © by Yusef Komunyakaa. Reprinted from *Pleasure Dome* (Wesleyan University Press) by permission of the author.

"Titanic" by Leadbelly, words and music by Huddie Ledbetter, edited by John and Alan Lomax TRO—Copyright © 1936 (renewed) Folkways Music Publishers, Inc., New York. Reprinted by permission.

"After His Athletic Father's Death" copyright © 1986 by Charles Levendosky. Reprinted from *Hands and Other Poems* by Charles Levendosky (Point Rider's Press, 1986) by permission of the author.

"Baby Villon" copyright © 1991 by Philip Levine. Reprinted from *New Selected Poems* by Philip Levine by permission of Alfred A. Knopf, a division of Random House, Inc.

"The Right Cross" copyright © 1992 by Philip Levine. Reprinted from *What Work Is* by Philip Levine by permission of Alfred A. Knopf, a division of Random House, Inc.

"Shadow Boxing" copyright © 2001 by Philip Levine. Reprinted from *First of the Month* by permission of the author.

"To a Fighter Killed in the Ring" copyright © 1967 by Lou Lipsitz. Reprinted from *Cold Water* by Lou Lipsitz (Wesleyan University Press, 1967) by permission of the author.

"Epigrams" by Lucilius, translated by Humbert Wolfe. Reprinted from *Others Abide* by Humbert Wolfe, Ernest Benn, Ltd.

"The Time Is Two, Not Three" copyright © 1962 by Norman Mailer. Reprinted from *Deaths for the Ladies (and Other Disasters)* (Putnam) by permission of the author.

Selection from *The Setup* by Joseph Moncure March copyright © 1928 by Covici, Friede, Inc. Copyright © renewed 1956 by Joseph Moncure March. Reprinted by permission of Crown Publishers, a division of Random House, Inc.

"Joe Louis Blues" by Carl Martin, 1935. Text provided by Rounder Records Corp., Cambridge, Massachusetts, 2001.

From *The Everlasting Mercy*: "Wood Top Fields" copyright © 1923 by John Masefield. Reprinted by permission of The Society of Authors, the literary representative of the Estate of John Masefield.

"Fist Fighter" copyright © by Dan Masterson. Reprinted from the *Ontario Review* 57 (fall/winter 2002–2003) by permission of the author.

"He's in the Ring" by Memphis Minnie McCoy copyright © 1935 by Universal-Duchess Music Corp. (BMI). All rights reserved. Reprinted by permission.

"The Nonpareil's Grave" by M. J. McMahon. Reprinted from *Sprints and Distances,* edited by Lillian Morrison (Thomas Y. Crowell Co., New York, 1965), with the following note appended: "Jack Dempsey the Nonpareil, a Brooklyn boy, was a middleweight champion of the late 19th century noted for his gameness. He died young. The poem was first printed anonymously in the Portland Oregonian, December 10, 1899. As a result of it, his friends raised money for a tombstone, and the poem now appears on it."

"Sonny Liston" copyright © by Jay Meek. Reprinted from *The Week the Dirigible Came* by Jay Meek (Carnegie-Mellon University Press, 1976) by permission of the author.

"The Seventh Round" by James Merrill copyright © 2001 by the Literary Estate of James Merrill at Washington University. Reprinted from *Collected Poems* by James Merrill, edited by J. D. McClatchy and Stephen Yenser, by permission of Alfred A. Knopf, a division of Random House, Inc.

"Sonny Liston" copyright © 1992 by E. Ethelbert Miller. Reprinted from *Thinker Review* 1.1 (summer 1992) by permission of the author.

"Irises at Ringside," an excerpt from "Iris," copyright © 2001 by John Minczeski. Reprinted from *Circle Routes* by John Minczeski by permission of the author and the University of Akron Press.

"Undefeated Heavyweight, 20 Years Old" copyright © by Joyce Carol Oates and The Ontario Review, Inc. Reprinted from *The Time Traveller: Poems* by Joyce Carol Oates (The Ontario Review, Inc., 1989) by permission of the author.

"'Angel Firpo' Waltz" copyright © 1923 by Salomon Pacorah, published by Salomon Pacorah, New York, 1923.

"Boxers Hit Harder When Women Are Around" copyright © 1939 by Kenneth Patchen. Reprinted from *The Collected Poems of Kenneth Patchen* by permission of New Directions Publishing Corp.

1 Corinthians 9:25–27 (St. Paul) is reprinted from The Small Group Study Bible (Carol Stream, IL: Tyndale House, 1995).

"To Let Go" copyright © 1984 by Michael Pettit. Reprinted from *American Light* (University of Georgia Press, 1984) by permission of the author.

"Olympia 7" and "Olympia 11" from *Odes of Pindar,* translated by Richmond Lattimore, copyright © 1947. Reprinted by permission of the University of Chicago Press.

"Joe Louis Is the Man" by Joe Pullum, 1935. Text provided by Rounder Records, Corp., Cambridge, Massachusetts, 2001.

"Petite Kid Everett" and "White Hope" copyright © by Ishmael Reed. Reprinted by permission of the author.

"None but Himself Can Be His Parallel" copyright © by John Reynolds. Reprinted from *Boxiana* (1824).

"No, No" copyright © by Yannis Ritsos. From *Petres Epanalipses Kinklithoma* (Stone, Repetitions, Railings) by Yannis Ritsos (Athens, Greece: Kedros, 1972). Translated by Scott King. Reprinted by permission of Scott King.

"Dead Shepherd's Hut" copyright © by Don Schofield. Reprinted from *Approximately Paradise* by Don Schofield (University Press of Florida, 2002) courtesy of the University Press of Florida.

"Steel Chin" copyright © by Peter Serchuk. Reprinted from the *North American Review* by permission of the author.

Copyright © 1951 by Charles Scribner's Sons. Reprinted by permission of Scribner, a division of Simon and Schuster, Inc.

"Punch-Drunk" copyright © 1985 by Michael Waters. Reprinted from *Anniversary of the Air* by Michael Waters (Carnegie-Mellon University Press, 1985) by permission of the author and Carnegie-Mellon University Press.

"Boxing Lesson" copyright © 1999 by Charles Harper Webb. Reprinted from *The Laurel Review* by permission of the author.

"King Joe (Joe Louis Blues)" copyright © 1991 by Richard Wright. Originally published in *New Letters* 38.2 and reprinted from *Richard Wright Works* (Viking Press, 1991) by permission of *New Letters* and the Curators of the University of Missouri–Kansas City and John Hawkins and Associates, Inc.

"Boom Boom Mancini" by Warren Zevon copyright © 1987 by Zevon Music. All rights reserved. Reprinted by permission.

"Suck It Up" copyright © 1996 by Paul Zimmer. Reprinted from *Crossing to Sunlight: Selected Poems* (University of Georgia Press) by permission of the author and the University of Georgia Press.

Robert Hedin is the author, translator, and editor of fifteen volumes of poetry and prose, most recently *The Old Liberators: New and Selected Poems and Translations*. He has been awarded fellowships from the National Endowment for the Arts, the McKnight Foundation, the Bush Foundation, the Minnesota State Arts Board, and the North Carolina State Arts Council. He has taught at Sheldon Jackson College, the Anchorage and Fairbanks campuses of the University of Alaska, St. Olaf College, Wake Forest University, and the University of Minnesota. He is the founder and director of the Anderson Center for Interdisciplinary Studies in Red Wing, Minnesota.

Michael Waters is a professor of English at Salisbury University on the Eastern Shore of Maryland. His volumes of poetry include *Parthenopi: New and Selected Poems; Green Ash, Red Maple, Black Gum; Bountiful; The Burden Lifters; Anniversary of the Air; Not Just Any Death;* and *Fish Light*. He is also the editor of *Contemporary American Poetry* (with A. Poulin Jr.); *Selected Poems* by A. Poulin Jr.; and *Dissolve to Island: On the Poetry of John Logan*. He has been a recipient of a fellowship from the National Endowment for the Arts, several Individual Artist Awards from the Maryland State Arts Council, and three Pushcart Prizes. He has taught in the creative writing programs at Ohio University and the University of Maryland and has been Visiting Professor of American Literature at the University of Athens, Greece, as well as Banister Writer-in-Residence at Sweet Briar College in Virginia.